Nobody Asked For This

Charly Cox

ONE PLACE. MANY STORIES

HQ
An imprint of HarperCollinsPublishers Ltd
1 London Bridge Street
London SE1 9GF

www.harpercollins.co.uk

HarperCollins Ireland
Macken House, 39/40 Mayor Street Upper,
Dublin 1 D01 C9W8

This edition 2023

1
First published in Great Britain by
HQ, an imprint of
HarperCollinsPublishers Ltd 2023

Copyright © Charly Cox 2023

Charly Cox asserts the moral right to be
identified as the author of this work.
A catalogue record for this book is available
from the British Library.

ISBN: 9780008591601

MIX
Paper | Supporting
responsible forestry
FSC™ C007454

This book is produced from independently
certified FSC™ paper to ensure responsible
forest management.

For more information visit:
www.harpercollins.co.uk/green

Printed and bound in the UK
using 100% Renewable Electricity at
CPI Group (UK) Ltd, Croydon, CR0 4YY

To my grandfather, all of this is for you –
even the bits that would've made you wince.

To Charlotte, despite it all, you lived.
You lived BIG and you lived true and with all the
hope in the world, you'll continue to for many years.
A hardback!!! Love, you from the future.

Contents

Nobody Asked For This

Introduction

None of this book should exist.
I know, like you, time changes who we are, but it is only now writing this I realise the extent to which this statement is true.

This is a collection of works written through some of the worst days of my life, periods that I vowed wouldn't last long enough to become a memory – let alone a poem.

All of this is evidence of those days, a morose alibi.
It's really hard to read them back. Yes, I did feel that. Yes, I did think that. Yes, those people did make me feel and think those things. It's hard to read this book knowing that it has all come from me. Knowing that I felt that way. Knowing that if I'd had it my way, most of it would be blank pages.

This book is formed of three collections. It is all writing that had acted as a lifeline for most of my life, written in secret, kept in diaries and hidden files with no intention of ever seeing the light of day. The earliest poem in this book was written when I was 14. I had planned to be dead two weeks after it had been written. It was originally published in *She Must Be Mad* when I was 22. I was sitting on the floor of my ex-boyfriend's kitchen when I found out that this collection was going to be published. It was a hideous and abusive relationship that I saw no end to unless I, myself, ended. I always thought he'd end up killing me, which could have been preferable to me killing myself; it made it seem less like I'd given up.

My second collection, *Validate Me,* was written when I was 23, during a bipolar manic high and a subsequent breakdown that I foolishly fought through, on bad advice, so I could do a book tour. I was given awards, ambassadorships, I went on holidays, I had dinner with my family – I did so many things whilst also suffering. That's the cool thing about illness: the right people can be a medical distraction, briefly.

Then, there is the new work that forms the final chapter of this book. An opportunity that came when I was soon to turn 27 – a date that had loomed large in my mental calendar for most of my life. I couldn't help but laugh at the timing.

Entangled with the worst days of my life were the best ones. The dates, the dancing, the simply sitting with a coffee and a cigarette people watching. The falling in love, the doing nothing. Those moments were allowed to flourish and grow because I always had an innate knowing – like the feeling that some women shrill about how 'I always KNEW I was born to be a stay-at-home mummy to little Freddy!' (Shut up, love – you were born privileged, not maternal) – that I was born to die in my twenties.

There's a signed letter in my GP's office that we wrote up when I was 17. It says, *I agree to quit smoking by the age of 30.* My GP said that, before I was 30, I could do whatever I liked as long as it kept me alive. After that, I was an idiot to continue doing anything that didn't consider my body as well as my brain. I signed that thing with such joy, a smile in my eye. It was a void contract. I would get to **churlishly** cheat my health for the rest of my days, because I'd be dead well before then. I knew then that I'd be gone before my twenty-seventh birthday.

Suicidal ideation is such that it feels incredibly concrete, even if it's future ideation. It also feels as though you've delved into a crystal ball and carved out what you need. It also feels really heavy and horrid and yet also numb and like nothing at all. Suicidal ideation is such that whatever shape it takes, you believe it. And, until a few months ago, I believed I'd never make 27. It felt as though, if I were a dog, you'd do the right thing and put me to sleep at that age. It felt too, in my bipolar mania, that it'd be fitting for me to die with the other artists. I am 27 as I write this. I have lived a decade longer than my 14-year-old self would ever have put the little money she had on living to. And I'm also happy to be here.

I'm living in a flat, on the same street as the primary school that I attended, with a man who I love, who I know loves me, navigating bipolar, navigating my finances, navigating what on earth it means to live – as that is clearly what I've chosen to do. I am also grieving my grandfather, who was my best friend in the entire world. It is bittersweet to have found a man I know he'd love, when he is no longer here, but sweet all the same to be here at all to tell this man all about my grandfather.

I have no idea how long this happiness will last, no idea what breaks of sanity or clarity or peace I'll be awarded. All I know is that I am so glad this book exists and I hope, if you're considering your own closing pages, that it might convince you otherwise, that it might show you that two truths are allowed to co-exist, even if one is that you absolutely want to die and the other is that you know deep down there is hope. The challenge is not living another day, but distracting yourself well enough to find yourself looking through the proof and alibis, trying to work out how a decade has gone by. Sometimes, you have to thrive in surviving.

It's been the best and worst decade, and the only one I've known as an adult. Jesus, I've not gone through it graciously, but gratefully, thank you – whether you're reading me for the first time or you've been here since the first ride, I'm here because of you. This is a collection that proves I lived, that's given to you, hoping you will too.

Keep fighting the good fight. I'll be trying alongside you.

Nobody

Asked For This

Nobody Asked For This

On the tube I am shivering
Face dripping with dew drops
Fingers tingling ankles clicking
Eyes on the moving tunnels
Waiting for them to stop
Meditation in my ears
But my brain keeps on spinning
Praying this new medication won't flop

A man swings from the poles
Tattered paper cup
He pushes an apology as he begs not to push his luck
Commuters push past and get off
An older woman rummages in her pocket
Only an offering of lost buttons and dust
A younger woman sucks her teeth and shouts
'Where is your humility?
He could be any one of us'
We all dissolve in the silence
Good enough to be the salt-in-water
Given to make the poisoned throw up
Still, no one coughs up
No one can stand the weight
Of the truth
We all sit complicit in his invisible
Life he didn't choose
Not our problem
And we've got it bad too
Not that kind of bad
But bad in its own way still
It just doesn't look the same as his
Swaying as our heads smack the partition

Thinking about the world, thinking how
Nobody asked for this
Whatever this is
Nobody asked for this

My brows are so bored of being furrowed
They've grown acne where the follicles meet
It's easier to look startled and wide-eyed
Than it is to let my disdain get to know my crow's feet
I've been thinking too much about the woman murdered by
      the park on the street
That we used to climb into after dark and drink whiskey neat
I've been thinking too much about how it could've been us
How it nearly was me
Not in that park or on that street
But give or take five or six times now
The trauma memory that doesn't remember
Is less of a hindrance and more of a treat
Five or six times maybe seven
But we can't agree on what counts
So I don't speak
I just spend too much time thinking about the woman
      murdered by the park on the street
Claw at my face
Pressurise the pimple
Feel the heat and bite of pain
Until it dribbles down my face
And bleeds
My knuckles relax into fists
Nobody asked for this
Whatever this is
Nobody asked for this

Chocolate digestives and household goods
Want us to know that they care
Loo cleaner, cosmetics and stuff for your hair
Daytime TV and posters on buses
Desperate to tell us they know what the fuss is
To tell us it's normal, this kind of despair
To tell us it's fine that we all ruminate
That we have doubts and regrets and nightmares
To tell us the truth that we already knew
That we're human and sometimes it's tough
To tell us the truth that we already knew
That currently everything's fucked
I'm frightened people will start to believe
They're as ill as me
HELLO I WAS HERE FIRST
Don't clog the line
It was just too much wine
The economy is a state
Your exams are just soon
HELLO I WAS HERE FIRST
Still queuing finding stuff to do
That isn't killing myself
Don't let them make you believe
Your brain isn't yours to keep
Don't become as drugged up as me
Have a minute to breathe
Maybe have a minute to scream and hiss
Open your eyes and let me tell you
Nobody asked for this
Whatever this is
Nobody asked for this

There are three women in the changing room
Shouting over the top

As their children run circles around the shop
One's huffing about bingo wings
The other says her husband calls out her mum tum
When she cries he says it's just banter
The one in the middle shouts
'At least you don't have cancer,
But God I could do with a virus'
Before she can finish her kid puts a hand to
His face and starts bawling
She bends down in her pants
Starts to tell him a story
About how some men prefer skinny women
Her mate interjects 'BORING!'
'BUT mummy please don't die'
All he'd heard was 'TERMINAL'
The rest of us browsing
Look at the dresses thinking 'Just burn it all.'
The room is depressing as hell
I felt fine as I'd entered
Now I'm caught in the swell
Of a child learning to hate its body
The way we hate them as well
The room is depressing as hell
It's filled with kids
Filled with impressionable minds
Perfectly good limbs
And us
Feeling guilty, feeling sad, feeling unworthy
Feeling inches of ourselves, feeling imperfect
Feeling like kids
Searching

Nobody asked for this
Whatever this is
Nobody asked for this

We are born with so much
That depletes without notification
Born with a pure hunger
That grows septic with satiation
It's sold
We are born with so much
And grown into less
Grown and brought up
Hammered through tests
That only make sense
To those who want to punish
Their parents
By punishing their children
By becoming a variant
Of turmoil they existed
We are nothing more
Than roots twisting and twisting
Desperate to stand tall
Desperate to survive our soil
Do it proud
Bathe in the sun

Nobody asked for this
Nobody at all
Yet here we all are grateful and frightened
Searching for meaning
In a gift
Nobody asked for this
Nobody at all
Yet here we all are trying to save it
Fight for freedom and buy into being a slave to it
Nobody asked for this
And even if we did
We probably couldn't afford it.

Baby Angel

I've been grounded for too long
Unable to feel that bad people do bad things
As soon as I elevated the need for seeing the good in you
I sprouted wings.

~~Byron~~ / **Wild at Heart**

If our tongues were speaking the same language
Twisting to the same dance
Carelessly licking a mist of arousal
Why do we not leave
With the same taste in our mouths?

You pick my drinks and I picked up the bill
Courting opposites, caught in emotional deficits
What a pointless privileged thrill
I wanted power, you wanted saving
I wanted wild at heart
Darling, you were lazy.

You did buy me flowers once
But you closed your eyes in bed
When I asked to have a drink waiting
You did a line without me instead
You ruined the first sunny day
Told me you dreamt about your ex
You cleaned your records, forgot your teeth
No one could be more perplexed
Than me
Who prayed too long for things to change
Of course.

All you saw was a woman on her knees.

Attach
Location

I don't want to do you down
I know you're capable
I know 'like me' you're solid
You could knee any man in the groin

I hate that to love you
I have to be certain
Better than a flip of a coin
A text must consolidate the night
No – *I had the best time*
Locations shared and *did you get home alright?*

~~Lean~~ / How Convenient

You like us silent
Until we are
So I own the space as though your racing thoughts cannot
     compete with the breath my closed mouth can hold

Nothing

Wet eyes and a grab of cuffs
A sigh, a leg cross, a huff
But I offer nothing
Watch you fall flat
You like us silent
Until we are
And you deserve exactly
That.

Boys

I wish they knew what we were giving up
Before they told you of their anxiety
Their fear of commitment
Their ex-girlfriend scars
Their desire to keep things simple

Do you know how long I could spend without paying
      for dinner
The A&Rs who I could blindly compliment for a pint
The grim but pure thrill of male friends staring at my cleavage
The pop stars who secretly want to fuck me
The barmen who'd die to
The white van men I could just hop in with

My own hands who know exactly where and for how long,
      without frigid fidget or a sigh of exasperation

I wish they knew what we were giving up
When they suggested seeing us under their exact terms
Was a hell we might contain them in.

LOVE

I always thought the problem was me
That I was too much
That I had too much love
But I've changed so much
Since I wasn't enough
And the thing that's withstood
The thing I leave with every time
The thing I walk in with blind
Is love
Problems aside
Because I am here only once
It's not that I am me
It is me who is love.

Anti-funeral

Party bunting as white flags
Balloons red like sirens
Let's celebrate my life
Before I'm too tired.

Singstar Sleepovers

We skip past the monoliths of us
Erected in a rose slur of
'Can you believe we survived that night?'
We laughed until our wrongs were right
We laughed in horror, in anger, in spite of
The people we feared we were becoming
Grown from adolescent longing
To be grown ups
Newsagents who knew us not by name but
'Pretty girl' dressed up to be much older
Now know us as sisters, we consider ourselves
     haggard spinsters
In our twenties
Still buying Monster Munch and cheap plonk
We still skip along
Past sirens and McDonald's trucks
The sweet hash air and friendly drunks
Careful not to step on cracks
Still soft for luck and kismet hacks
We are still those little girls
Delighting in playing adults to the world

There is pause in it all
In the Sunday market
In the walls our names are scratched
On the road our postcode matched
In the faces we've never seen before
In the foreign fragrances and the Kilburn drawl
In the church doorways we have kissed
Outside the pubs we've screamed and hissed
In the cafés we've soaked our souls
In crisped-up fatty bacon rolls

In the Christmas lights that never worked
In the old neighbour's smirks
There is pause.
Where we will always be ageless
Dreamers, learners, hopeful souls with patience
To feel home

We've stumbled all of Soho's streets
We've snuck in and devoured Mayfair's treats
We've sat swinging legs long on Camden Lock
We've marvelled at Shoreditch, gone south
And more north
We've napped on tubes
And strangers too
And ferried our way back on our trusty Bakerloo
Back home
Back to NW

I was birthed in this swell
Not quite Ladbroke Grove or Maida Vale
I came alive, took breath to find
No matter how many times we'd leave we'd always come
        back and find
Each other

We are still those little girls
You and here and this part of me –
My world.

I Said I Didn't Want Kids, I Lied

I stood killing time in a sample sale
You reached out your hand
Your mother smiled 'Percy'
I said 'No! Don't tell me his name,
this is already too much for me.'
But you gripped on anyway

I sat flicking through the Sunday supplements
Your eyes met mine and stared on forever
Your mother's friend brought you over
I said 'THERE SHE IS!' when I wanted to ask
'Can I hold her?'
But you played peek-a-boo instead

I day drank with friends talking about rape
You waddled over with a grin
Your dad let you explore
I said 'Won't be a moment' and they all watched me
on the floor
Talking to you the way my heart sings to me

I live every day as a mother
You all see it in me
Whoever's care you're in knows it too
I know it too
Just not yet
It takes more than want, heart, luck and privilege
It takes knowing you can offer a village
And I can't even afford my rent.

Gen Zzzzzzz

Having a time of my life that I wish was a different kind
Likely more useful if I had the time
To see that this time in my life
Could be the time of my life
If the pressure of that didn't make me want to die
What a time to be alive
Jesus Christ.

Lazing with the Dog

There is a muchness to you
No sad song story that I recite
Speaks too much for you,
Too tough to decipher
Nothing your hazel-coloured shapes
Have seen in their life are

As much as you
The touch of you is often accidental
A paw-grazed thigh and a licked nose is a fundamental
Motion-cum-gesture that spurs my morning happy
I was never sure of motherhood but for you I will care gladly
I will learn a new set of vowels
And how to shout them madly

When you chew on my socks or respond to my cuddles flatly

Half-whimper, half-yawn we mirror each other in a daze
Lying in the splinters of summer, warming our backs in the
Sun's embrace

Together we know nothing more
Than the excited sound of Mum's keys in the door.

Our love is as new as the day and as old as you remember
And in that uncertain parameter all my body feels is

Splendour.

Chicken Little

They say it'll snow next summer
Flakes flailing their limbs in horror
Armageddon's closer
Hell has done a runner
From the bottom of the earth and met us here
Those closer to the ground can smell it
And it stings their ducts with tears
The gods with their complexes
Cackle down at dripping necks
Like they've got nothing to fear
I wonder what hole they'll leave in the ground
As they fall from the sky
When we're too busy to catch them.

Powers

I am a witch
For I am a mad woman
Whose spells she can't control
Frighten the world
Even when they could heal it.

~~Jack~~ / Skip to the Good Bit

Loved you from the depths of me
As you clutched to the end of me
I never thought I'd get a chance
To kiss you and tell you all that you were
Blindly ignoring the simple romance
We were kids
Breaking into waterfalls
Chasing horses in the rain
I can still hear our playlist playing
My heart still aches the same
We got as far as the electrics box
Just up the road from your house
Spitting secrets and splitting spliffs
Till no words came from our mouths

We should have kept us there
How cruel to free us from the frame
Old photos now sullied with the truth
You never felt the same.

Artists

Inconsiderate
I knew you weren't different
This time I won't shoulder it
I won't mould you to a lover for you to find the words to
write about another
This story is mine
You don't get the girl this time
You don't get to find a safe space kissing my neck
You don't get to hide or seek me missing you, a wreck

I know hurt people hurt people
But frankly I don't deserve you
You're head and shoulders above the rest
You're an answer not a test
So hold your hands up, you're inconsiderate
I slam my own down, I won't shoulder it

So many strings to my bow it's become a violin
Plucking up the courage to stop crying
Hanging back to not scream is a discovery
I'm a bitch in recovery.

Move On

Yawning just to cry
Grazing skin to show I tried
Doing everything to fall
Breaking the legs off my own stool
Call me a loser
A liar and a fraud
Run to come see how I've grown tall
Swim but not to save me
Because now I can walk on water
I can't drown now I've felt it all

Swim but not to save me.

Single

I think we're two broken Pringles at the bottom of the tube
Hiding from a hand that's too big to reach us
Tessellating for safety
All salty.

Premature Obituary

I immortalised you before I knew anyone could go
How did I know
That every scrap of you was so precious
That no one should live without it
That they can't
Because for as long as I'm alive
For as long as my friends breathe
For if I have children
All your stories forever weave
How did I know
To love you in a past present tense
Was the way you'd never leave
The final weeks you seemed at peace
Did you always know
You could slip off whenever you fancied
Your presence still a tease
No one could ever know
Other than me
That you'd be so smug secretly

Thank you for always trusting me.

Laurence

Ponytails tied like tongues keeping messy secrets
Medusa's back with the women on her street
Serrating lips in ways you asked me not
To when you kissed me and I gave you teeth
'Bash me with one or the other'
You pulled from my mouth like you couldn't feel what
    passion means

I reek with this morning's sweat
Fired in confident glow, no regret
Smoking cigarettes furiously like I did in your bed
Still stuck in a gaze with your little boy's head
Framed, keeping an eye on us as we slept

I'm not here to grow you down
Regress over lunch with your mother
Redress me before you kiss another
Bash me with one or the other
I'm not here to grow you down
The comedy you swear as truth is only spittle in her mouth
That tastes like when I was around
Seven hours before now

I reek with passion and this morning's sweat
Fired in confident glow, no regret
Smoking cigarettes furiously like I did in your bed
Still stuck in a gaze with your little boy's head
Framed keeping an eye on us as we slept

Lines that weren't marked to cross
But that's all we were made to be
Lines that weren't marked to cross.

Just lines of forged and forced humility
Scrape your chair back, we can all see
You caressing her hair down just like you did with me.

You Can't Hurt Me Anymore

Oh God I wish you knew
How painful loving you
At first sight
Every time
Has become

How long it's taken me to see
You're at war with love
When I've only just begun
What a waste of warmth and intention
On someone's angry son

You're at war with love

I have only just begun.

'Murica

Change isn't scary when you're holding a weapon
What a way to think of a heart
What a thing to threaten

Safety-catch lies
This information isn't knowledge
Intuition is what we should've wanted

This is how it should've been told
This is why women grow wise
And boys never grow old.

A Letter to my Unborn Child

He decides his future
Says
He can't handle you
Thinks it'll be better
Without your voice

My darling

Rejoice

The only thing I'll push on you
Is that your presence is joy

Anyone who suggests it's something else
Have a word with yourself

Then let him think twice.

I Kept the Window Locks to Deter Buyers

To lock away your screams and hurt
To push the window open wide
To see the neighbours dancing naked
To watch teddy bears fly

How dare they take away our house
To make into their new home
Without the justice of inheritance
To leave us with what should be left
Dead without a headstone

You can seal away the damp and rot
But I'll always have the only lock
On the haunting that this place forgot.

Take Your Medicine

I am a walking experiment
I am bad science and chemicals
A test tube with legs
The world goes in
And I come out
And it hurts.

Not My Usual

Perhaps a type set
A stereotype
A preference, a want
Is the furthest indication of what we truly need
Otherwise how would I have come to learn
Mayonnaise mixed with English mustard on chips
Realism on climate anxiety
Hedonism, sex-parties
Could be of interest

I speak English and I smoke
Run rings round parties
Much like the ripples of cellulite that circle a feast of me
I am black-cross-in-a-box-for-you
Yet blue double ticks are what I want from you

Perhaps a type set
A stereotype
A preference, a want
Is the furthest indication of what we truly need
Otherwise how would you have known I got home safely
After we denied our on-paper passions
And instead spent all night kissing on the street?

We Looked Different in our Photos

The second from the top has the highest markup
Men on dates don't wish to look cheap
So we order from the very top
As though our frugality is cultured
As though we are more expensive than the third
We climb down the bottle
We shudder furniture closer
We pull blankets around this wintered spring
We
We
We
Strangers speak to us in 'we'
Not you
Not me
Our tongues climb from our lips
Our shoulders shudder at first kiss
Our bodies pulled close like blankets
Wrapped like winter, hopeful as spring

Unlikely to meet the summer as we
Content within the pendulum swing.

You're Terribly Unworthy

I couldn't love you more, it's true
I haven't the capacity to imagine it
As for now, right now, all I know is you
I have known others
I have loved them too
In fact I have been in love so many times
That whilst this fertile ground is ready
It won't flourish, simply can't
Because *It* has never known what it feels to be loved too
It is hope that rakes it back to hope
Parting atoms back to ground
If only hope would let *It* settle
So the seeds of salted experience had a chance to sprout
I could love you so much more,

Thank God I don't know how.

Dougie

You light up as I smoke the breath out of you
Delicate and present
As though to devour is the same as to savour
No peace in my mind is left un-whispered to
What could be made of this other than love?
Even if it's not forever
Other than something so safe
So crave-worthy
So gentle as it is sobering
To the already sober
A tight grasp, steady
That still pushed me over
For you

How sacred not to feel scared
So full in my body, so bared
So taken, so tied
By the woman who shouted
'REMEMBER YOU'RE THE PRIZE'
As I left the pub alone to get to yours.
I wasn't at dinner, I lied
But that's the only time
There's nothing sexy admitting my Saturday night plan was a
        scheduled-in cry

To stare you down like this
Capturing your features like a criminal
Crossing free fingers to not witness a line-up
Crossing lines into kisses, ignoring the subliminal
Space and language of such deep hurt
When did the bar fall so low
That being held so naturally

Feels so gracious
That you've not shown me your worst

Is this a stone's throw from healing
Shattering the fragile glass pain of grieving
That the woman who leaves tonight
Is no longer me
My worth not this – nor is it lost
But then, did I ever really know who she was?

A one-time wonder of thunder
Bright enough to not need the storm
Every late-night phone call – five hours long
Every wait for a reply – five hours long
Every want for something more settled
More concrete on butterfly wings
Crashed away

Your eyes light up as I taste your nicotine gum
Thoughtless in delight yet still with a head full
Brought to each other with a divine right not to settle
No ending, no real crescendo
I just hope you think of me and smile
As I do you, when I wait for the boil of the kettle.

Back at Jon's After That Persian Restaurant on Romilly Street

Your eyes a different colour
To what I'd seen at dinner
The whites a tinge of watered red
Bright globes of blue swimming in Ribena

Mine hellbent on melting like ice cubes on the surface
Floating waiting to dissolve
Into the words you stutter nervous

But they stare you back, all dumb not dim
To project the shadow of your reflection in
The words black and brilliant on the ceiling

Answers laid out without a question
I'd felt it all for weeks, every sentiment above me
But there was absolutely nothing
To have prepared the right response,
Knowing that you love me.

Remember When We Broke Up Before We Started?

He's brushing his teeth and I'm smoking

It's been three nights and three half-days
Splits of sunshine and licks of tobacco
The kitchen table is a mess
And so is everything else before I get back home
He froths minty at the mouth
I puff out smoke
I've always felt like the bloke
Who is told to leave the bar
Before it all goes too far

Before someone ends up crying

It's been three nights and three half-days
Worth we'd never thought we'd conjure
Hangs like broken string lights on the balcony
Few filaments want to twinkle at the alchemy
The others stopped tired and we shrug
As though the wrong punctuation is better than none

I don't leave jewellery on the bedside table
Because I know I'll be back again.

Resilience

The hit, the crack
The full body blow
Your body withstanding the most incredible pain
With no victory to show
But the life you have that grows
That whimpered wrong at the thought
Of needing the person you once were go

The bamboo stick, the green thin twine
The legs that had never quite been mine
The plant food pack, the gardening gloves
The unsure smile at a half-grown love
Not yet in summer's glory
You can't believe spring has passed so quickly
You can't remember that winter robbed you of leaves
The structures stripped away to give your roots a
        chance to simply
Breathe
Unknotted from the kindly shackles that were tied to you and
        the world from birth
Now it's just you and the earth
Ready and willing
To bloom something so innate
It startles you and makes others shake
It is your worth and it's roaring
Even in your silence
It is the stem of strength
That gives you breath

Resilience is a feast we are wise not to feed from
But a wildfire we cannot escape or be free from
It's the life in our solid bones

It's the blood for our blood
The scraps of soil on stones
That colours it unclean
It's the times we tried so hard to be nice
But came across mean
But knew what we meant
And inside felt so seen
That nothing can argue its way through the doors
Of our strength, of our sanity
Our worth – though it's flawed
And though the floor is a trap
That we often fall through
We land on our feet
Smile as though it's new
To hold ourselves steady
But the tricks and the traps
Are coded into our past life's diligence
We are born from woman
And we breathe fresh resilience.

Nothing is as strong as our forgotten nerve
The muscle that is our strongest reserve
The skin that healed before it was scored
The body we've wished was less that was always more
                    Than that
The resilience that holds us accountable
The force we feel that smacks us when we're doubtful
We can wake up again
And go through the same tired shit

The whole world is against us
And when we say it
The whole world is against us again
What is a game to play that you didn't want to

But losing

What is not winning worth until you test the fragility of the
   other players' choosing

What is being forced to bow down to others' assumed
   brilliance

If you can't stand straight and stare it down with resilience?

Falling in Love With Jon

To be anything but unsure feels not present
Feels conceited
Feels like a thick fat dribble of a lie
That's lubricating eyes before they're defeated
It feels as loathsome on the surface as hurt
Not asked for, not wanted, not deserved
It feels as alien as it feels home
As though home was on Saturn
As though the rings aren't drawn around me
But I've contained myself in my own pattern
Then this thing landed on a different planet
Welcomed me over
And there was nothing there but a view of the stars.

A Love
Like Grief

Consider the we who wandered without the other
The versions of us who drank and laughed
Who fought and shouted
Even though that wasn't who we were
Or who we are
Consider the nights on the sofa
Because they were easier

The quick us
The push and pull but push again us
The before us
The two wholes who were living as halves
Whenever we recite these times we laugh
In each other's faces
We are brand new

We've met before, it's certain
Not in the restaurant you paid for dinner
Not in the pub I paid for pints
Not in the days we chose to breathe the day
Not in the days that felt like nights
We are brand new

Every morning that I see your face
I love it like it's grief
Because the we that wandered
Wondered right
That we are whole in love's belief.

Learning How

Quite the unrequited consumed consummate pro
At falling down rabbit holes
Where love has no intention to grow
So familiar
Such comfort in its bittersweet
Of knowing the end before it's known as defeat
What trouble it would be to be happy
When this lonely has become its own cosy retreat
I couldn't possibly know how to be
But then yesterday morning I woke up to find
You were already up, leg bent round mine, smiling at me.

I Know You'd Love Him

Smiling is a funny kind of sadness
That robs the throb of a trembling lip
That thinks it's crying out laughter
Before it knows it's tears
It feels hopeless being happy
Without you here

I can't handle love anymore
Knowing you won't delight in it
Knowing you won't comment on the light
Of my lips
As I give you a kiss
And tell you all about it
I want to tell you all about it
Every little bit.

Unfinished

I daren't translate you into wobbled words
Daren't root you in a sentence
I dare not pretend each vignette you offer
Could be one poem when there's
So much more to bring light to,
And what potential and a delight to
Be this thing that is a wallop of a cliché
For you
I daren't be anything other than the love I transcend to
Every time I stop searching for language and just watch the
little things that you do.

Insight Timer

Weeks blur into afternoons
Punctuated only by taking it in turns
To watch the other sleep
Later and later each night
Or do the afternoons blur into weeks?
There's no longer much to be sure of
Only that I want to spend all this time
I used to want to keep.

Mental Hypochondria

So worried I'm lying
And really I'm fine
Guzzled in guilt
That pain is now numb
How do I know what is real and what's not?
When I search in my brain
All I find is rot.

Moving In

You unscrew furniture I built alone
Sort books I found an ego solace
Roll your boxers into drawers that have only seen my socks
Now unmatched on the floor
I grimace at Arcade Fire as you make us breakfast
My stomach hurts like it did when I was a child
I grab my thumbs in my fist, an old technique

This could be everything I ever dreamed of
If everything I touch wasn't trauma

I no longer need my hands to pray for us or you
Only to case around the wounds so I can breathe
To see us, two.

A Love Song for Someone Else

If we passed on the street
Would we take a second glance
If we could do this over
Would we jump at the chance
Are we the same people who fell hard for love?
I can't tell
Now that I know you so well

I know your favourite cities
I know your order at the bar
I know I'm your favourite face
I know the cure to your scars
I know your passport number backwards
I know your mother's greatest fears
I know the staccato of your footsteps
Telling me that you're near
I know everything so well, I learnt it all so fast
So why now do I worry about if this will last
What if the person of my future
Is no longer you from the past
I can't tell
Now that I know you so well

The bodies that we built together
Have the same voice
But now the worry of us here forever
Feels like a burden without a choice
If we made each other better, bigger
Have we outgrown the promise of our sell
I don't know who I was before
The me who knows you so well
How do we tell
The difference between?

Metal Mouth

It's not the end that tastes the same
It's the aching bones and throb
It's the waking need to drink
It's the startling desperate want
It's the desperate
Desperate
Want
To not
Think each end tastes the same
When we've still got what we've got

It's not the end that tastes the same
It's the fear of inadequacy
That sprints up veins in fingers
Having ignored its creep for weeks
It's no full moon, no period
A different cycle that knows more
That every high that's been this good
Has left me on the floor

It's not the end that tastes the same
It's just my tongue in my mouth
How can anything taste different?
When my saliva has always been soured?

Six Feet Under

Is it crude to think of you sound asleep
With your pockets full of titbits that we chose
With your arms down straight
Polished shoes and pointed toes
Your skin as soft as when I last stroked it
Still untouched by worms or moss
A snore whose echo swells the wood
Dreaming so many dreams your mind is lost
So lost it stumbles into mine
So lost that when I close my eyes
I'm dreaming warm cuddled next to you
Is it crude that when I go to bed each night
I pretend I'm six feet under, too?

Up, Down, Left Or Right

With enough pressure
It will explode into passion
With enough forgiveness
In its softest form
I might break inhuman shape
Tear trauma out of my jeans
Like nothing ever happened before

Beaconsfield Station

We lost our heads that day
Every body dismembered
In some way

I see you all the time
In my dreams you arrive with a thwack
A crunch of tracks
There you are
Just,
Back
One arm
Maybe more
I wasn't sure
My eyes were black

I should've stayed in bed
Should've walked up to the shop
Should've brushed my teeth with haste
Left to scrub toothpaste off my top
Should've left my keys
Should've left my straighteners on
Left my gym gear out for the morning
Pushed my trainers for a run
Should've called my mum
Lists of things I should've done
Should've got there fifteen minutes early
Should've waited on the wrong side
Should've seen you walk in
Should've given you a smile
Should've asked you for the time
Should've given you some of mine

I think about the conversation
Police ringing someone's phone
As they butter toast
At your family home
Take a bite before the shock
Knocks their heart to stone

Countless trains I have missed
Headlights I've stared down
Countless tiptoes on the yellow line
Wishing I was no longer around
You took that thought away from me
Something I believed no one would ever do
I just wish that when you took it
It didn't take you too.

Hallucinating You

Memories are clearer now
Almost in front of me
I wonder if that's because I am so scared to lose them
Or that I only feel okay when I am fully back in them
I only worry that in this desperation
I am accidentally rewriting them
One last scent at a time.

Louise

How funny
I was thinking of you earlier as my stomach dropped
When he held a candle to my face and learnt my palms too early
I thought about you last night in bed
When I wriggled in pain as my mind wouldn't rest and I felt
    cystitis coming
I thought about you when I put my hand around the lid of
    my beta blockers after an espresso martini and my
    teeth caged
I thought of you when I babbled to a news reporter and said
    the word brilliant too many times and felt a fraud
I thought of you when I tucked my expensive T-shirt into my
    cheap denim skirt and felt bloated
I thought of you when I got too drunk at The Box and cried
    and told everyone I'd been assaulted
I thought of you when I asked for my stuff back and still felt
    sick, like the closure that I want is something that I don't
I thought of you when I sat in the football stands and wished
    I'd brought your son so he could tell me what was what
It's funny
I think of you in all the times I feel so desperately unseen
So desperately alone
The times I'm glad no one can hear the inside of my brain
But let myself believe you can
Because I know you'd understand
And I know you'd make me laugh
And I know it would all pass
And nothing else would truly matter but the thought of us
Discussing us
And how stupid we are
For feeling so unfair
In these feelings that we share.

Inheritance

In your physical absence
It seems as though I make clearer sense of me
The you in me
I work less to see your actions in my words
Or notice how the things that I enjoy
Are yours
Things I thought were commonplace
Common sense
Innate
Are things that only we have in common
Because you taught them to me
It's as though my whole life before was a lie
When you were here
I thought I was my own entire being
An individual
But now you are elsewhere
I realise I am all you
Elsewhere, not gone
For my arms and legs still move.

Father Figure

If we could hang about
We'd do it in a pub
I'd pick an expensive wine
You'd laugh that I knew my stuff
Order fish and chips if that's okay
Hope I'm paying but not mention anymore
We'd talk about disappointing men
How I don't deserve them
Chances are my prince has been born
Muse on The Range as a lifestyle not a store
We'd drink shandies and console each other
Talk about our dads and your brothers
We'd reminisce
Like we have the same things to miss
And you'd say 'why don't you just see him
He loves you hear him out'
But I'd do anything to hang with you
Rather than hang a man
That offers unconditional love
With an ounce of doubt.

New Daughter or Wife?

When you use forgiveness as a commodity
Beware of who will be bought
Beware of those who have been used
Who sell themselves on what they've been taught

By men like you.

When I look in your eyes I see my replacement
I'm searching for closure
Searching for breaks of pain in your story to humanise you

Perhaps this is flattery I can't afford

How odd to be born

Knowing I am not the worst of what I've done.

Survivors

We spray nice noise instead of trauma
Spit is caught from screen
Every tepid flirt
Is renounced to the softest scream
I tell you all about me
You verse a choice, the same
We learn everything about each other
But you'll never know his name.

pLeAsE dOn'T wRiTe PoEmS aBoUt Me!!

I know now
Something I vow
To value until my grave
Those who are fearful of being immortalised
Are not the ones you save

Don't let them die in your edits
Write their eulogy as soon as you can
Because only the guilty are frightened
Of seeing their own blood drip from your hands.

Why Aren't You Repulsed by Me?

A fear of you has settled in
I, unmoved
It's much like dust
You paralyse my inner knowing
When I think of us

It's not that you aren't perfect
Funny, familiar, kind
It's that you're all of those things
To me
You seem to like me
Most of the time

You listen to me ramble
Cook me dinner, don't cough at my smoke
There's no secret you've not yet handled
No distance you've pushed further
Even though we've been remote

This fear of you, it's strange to me
I love love for all it's worth
But I think perhaps I've said it before
When for you I've felt it first.

Friends
in Love

How to take a dive in a sea
That offers so much expanse to breathe
But so much underneath
That must exist too

How do you edge closer to the truth
That there is no other option
But to spend our lives side by side in contented silence
Or our lives in love
No island strong enough to cling to
If one of us wears out

We must either be each other's forever
Or each other's, forever
Paddling too feeble
A paddle useless as just one
Why would I endure the shock of cold
That could make the death of two
Who had already won?

Babies' Feet

They beat you up from the inside
Then you meet them on the outside
And the beating on the inside is now just pangs of
    missing them
Even though they're right in front of you.

Ali

We used to camp out on the grass
Pop out goals swathed like shrines
Painting from the spots in black
Begging stories from our eyes
They never really made much sense
Why would they
We were young
But there was always much more truth in us
Than when we were kicking footballs in the sun

The stars weren't much in north-west London
But spaceships often passed
As did flashes of a first-felt love
That we'd not remember if we were asked.

Pride

We excavate our hearts for space
To say
I love you
Knowing language for the feeling
Has been so hard to discover
It's fullness, richness, intoxicating
Too grand to take a single form
So it must take pride in every colour.

~~Max~~ / French House Fooling Around

It's not you it's me
Truly
I'm who turns me on
I'm the one who decided
What you said was right
Who forgot there was so much wrong
It's not you it's me
Proudly

Writing my own skin back
Praising and praying years back
You're teaching me to read
My mother tongue
I've never felt so young
And so grown up
You make me a woman for me
Getting off on what you know I now see
You make me a woman for me.

Validate Me

Introduction

Are you the friend that takes sweet secret gratification in others' failures? Do you like to indulge in delicious disastrous irony? How about oxymorons? Do you have a few moments to spare to flick through a book that warrants no need for more attention than a glance at your phone? Or perhaps – here's the clincher – are you a person that has a 4G connection and is currently alive on this here planet?

If you answered yes to any of the above, please take a seat whilst you sign away a few precious cells of your brain to the validation of my mental breakdown. A little scribble of thought with the tiny Argos pen you stole in your childhood is all I need. With that too take your own validation, you're a climate change warrior, that could've been single use. Can I get you anything? A dog meme? An old photo of Paul Danan off his tits? A Trump tweet to make you question what is left of this already heavy and futile opinion on life? Well, get up and get it yourself because I am currently circling around Praed Street, Paddington, London, dictating this into my phone having just strolled out of Accident and Emergency with little but an offer of self-sectioning and a plastic festival-like wristband with my name and date of birth on it as a keepsake. I am busy and now you are too, so Lady Gaga and Piers Morgan can wait, we have got a lot to try and decipher about how it got this far.

Nothing riles me more [this is a lie as you're about to read a book which is essentially a long list of things that rile me to the point of medication punctuated only by rhyme and the rare smatter of hope] than an introduction whereby the writer refers to the infancy of the book's process. It leaves me with a bored, bourgeois sour taste of someone else's self-importance, but as I've been hailed as an #instapoet I fear I owe it to some sanctimonious troll to exceed a slither of expectation. So let us suck the soured serotonin out of my life lemon.

I pre-empted this. I knew almost so certainly I was on the cusp of complete digital burnout that I pitched this collection thinking I was saving myself from it. Charly from the past, all omniscient, and evidently omnipotent, cackled her way through a Google doc, tripping over a cocktail of www.woes that she knew were exhausting but perhaps important and valid and witty, and hit send. Charly from the past but a few weeks later delighted at the idea of being able to use poetic licence for the first time in her sad, sad life. What fun! You need not sell the last fragment of your young and underdeveloped soul and past trauma! You can use FORESIGHT! And now Charly in the present is furiously walking to Marylebone station at 5am because her contactless card doesn't work so she can't get the tube and is desperately aware that everyone is staring at her in the night before's party dress, mascara on her chin and a hospital bracelet. She's also talking into her phone in third person, so I need not break this to tell you how far away from the grand dreams of poetic licence she is. This collection, albeit caricatured, is true. Some of it was written on grand spanking highs in expensive hotels in Los Angeles where I (ever the optimist in irony) searched for physical validation, a boyfriend, stardom and a good Instagram opportunity; some of it in bed wheezy on Venlafaxine, Propranolol and an algorithm that hates my content; some of it in Ubers and on trains; some of it to the soundtrack of the men in my local, little countryside pub; some of it leaving a hospital working out if I shouldn't have run away from it. But all of it was written on my phone and all of it is because of the curse of exactly that.

There. That's how we got here. This thing in my hand that stole all of my smarts so it could preface its own name with them.

Hello, my name is Charly Cox and I am code-dependent. So would you please, please just validate me.

Validate

Me

The Dinner Party

Regram the gifted
Who told it much better?
Who rehashed the clickbait much neater?
Who braved brevity
And got down on one knee
To marry an idea so desperate
Without meeting its parents?
Who cares for the source
When you can skim its matter of course
And still impress all of your friends?
They'd never dare question
Such a good-looking suggestion
For fear of not knowing enough
And having done the same.

Celebrity

I want the moon
I want the sky
I follow the stars
I want their shine

I want it all
All that's above me
I want nothing more
Than to be it and for them to love me

I want what I can't reach
I want all that I can see
I want the things that I can't touch
I want it all, I want so much!

I want! I want! I must! I must!

How foolish, silly, dumb and fucked
To salivate
To celebrate
Social divinity
When there's a piece already in me
What ignored-already fortune
What blinded, wasted luck.

Cary's Castle

You catwalk the bar
And head for the screen
Take off your sunglasses
A sigh a relief
Just mumbles of others
A curtain between
Sat entirely alone
Unmasked with huge swollen eyes
Feeling uncomfortably alive
Feeling finally seen
By no one but you
A sigh a relief
Finally seen
It's grim and it's snotty
It reeks of sweat and of sleep
It curdles within you
A rotten green pang
And then from out of the barrier
A stranger puts out his hand
You shrug off reluctant
He's killing your moment
But, actually, he's there
To properly show you it
'London!' his voice swells
'You must be an actress?'
Not quite, you reply, though this is definitely acting
'But your beauty, that accent, what's your success?'
I guess today I finally got out of bed
That's all there is
Everything else is a mess
'Kid,' he says, 'look,'
This guy is pulled straight from a film

'You've got yourself here
I saw you come over to hide, head bowed as you walked, I
	know that stride, you needed to talk,
And I'll give it to you straight
You don't need to smile for the room
But put one on your face
Because what you feel inside
Is the best art that you'll make
It's all yours to keep
But it's getting you down because you've been giving it out
Instead of giving it chance to ruminate
I'm so glad I wasn't grown up in the digital age
Because I've learned that it's all much too easy to fade
When you're forced to dine out on gesture
Giving meals for those who weren't meant to take.'

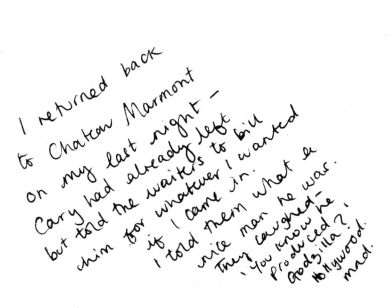

I returned back
to Chateau Marmont
on my last night –
Cary had already left
but told the waiters to bill
him for whatever I wanted
it I came in.
I told them what he was.
nice man he was.
They laughed –
'You know he
produced –
Godzilla?
Hollywood
mad.

Worth

It's not in the ether
Left to wriggle and writhe
It's not lost in your legs
Pouring out when they're lithe
It's not in your emails
It's not in your likes
It's out in your life
It's on the ground waiting
When you need to survive

Stories

They wore Shrimps
Ate a few
Passed around crystal glasses
Chinked, cheered and cherished
Until they fell on their arses
What a sight to behold

It was warm orange autumn
No greater deed than to
Fall back and relax
Cans of Stella, bags of crisps
BMXs and Vans and pillowed-up Eastpaks
What a sight to behold

She'd turned seven
There was cake
Balloons and party bags
They're making secret memories
One's they'd never think to brag
I wasn't invited
What a sight to behold
Though this one I couldn't see
Just left to imagine what I'd never have been told.

WHY WON'T YOU LIKE MY SELFIES??????

What I like the most
Is I know he never lies
His kindest vocabulary
Is locked in shrugs and sighs
Sweet loving eyes
That bind to mine
In honey
I sink down within it all
And let it all run off me
For as much as I could bathe
In all his unspoken compliments
Sometimes all I really want
Is for him to scream at me with confidence
To hit me that I'm stupid
To bash me that I'm smart
To strangle me until it's me who's mute
I'd take that as a start.

Monzo

Things of value used to last a lifetime
But now they're things that we regret
Feelings, cash, commodities
Mis-spent
Notified in a text.

All Reads Are Good

For the love of Christ, Keats and Rupi
For the love of the lonely
For love of the only
Words that make us safe
Pick up this book
Pick up another
Just find comfort for comfort's sake

Slate it, slant it, sling it back
Cast it stupid, naive, unpretty
But one man's 'pile of precocious shit'
Is still allowed to be a young girl's favourite ditty.

Toby

I miss you so terribly
The pain of which I need not study
To understand
All my human data enmeshed
Sprawling axes and climbing charts
Coloured bars and kisses crossed
You learn me constantly
Consistently
Always present like this feeling
I miss you so terribly
So terribly it's almost lovely
So terribly I feel deserving
So terrible so lovely to know
That whilst your love is seldom simple
Your voice on a call
Always feels like home.

Trolls

Carnivorous and hungry
They're always out on the prowl
Don't care that you're happy just want to know how
So they can pull it from your clutches
Steal a piece for their own
Fighting bare skin and knuckles
Euphoric?
Step away from your phone.

The Instructions They Forgot To Give

Behind every fear is a wish
Behind every wish is a dream
Behind every panic
Every stop, start and flat line
Every reshuffle and standby
Is purpose
And longing
Behind every hour of hard work and solitude
Is the making of hours of future and evolving
Behind the people you detest
Putting your moral alignment to test
Behind digital deliberation
Behind dating frustration
Behind overwhelmed feeling
Behind every half try at success

Is purpose

Behind the days you feel worthless

Is purpose

It's clichéd and disgusting
It's sickly sweet
It's improbable and unlikely
That it'll ever present itself as neat
No unambition is exciting
Nor is it worth achieving
Nor is living out your dreams
Only when you're sleeping
What nonsense is living

Only a reality that's disbelieving
Your desires
Waking day to day
Putting out your heart's wildfires
Denying its purpose
Making time for the exhausted surplus
Of becoming the imposter
Growing up your insecurities
And leaving your best qualities unfostered

Behind being angry at others who are better
Behind being comfortable with shrugging off 'whatever'
Behind losing yourself to a constant anxiety
Is a purpose that's screaming for you to wake up
And see that behind every fear is a wish
And behind every wish is a dream
And behind all the things that you feel are obstacles
Is simply you putting an excuse in-between.

Instagram Boyfriend

You would sit
Marsupial
In the pocket of my Kooples
Jacket
Ready to pounce
Unironic
Tripod and macro gadgets
At the sight of stucco houses
To shoot me cardboard cut-out
Beatles walk
And make me feel
Liked and skinny/
Nonplussed look to the left/
#pretty.

Bath

Wrapped up in bed sheets
Mummy denied
Toes tipping and dipping to song
My eyes staring straight through the ceiling
To rest in the sky
He hits keys practiced but not languid
I try not to cry
At all that I've become since I was last here
My tongue flat bitten under teeth that are still furred with beer
And pride

Escape should feel dream-like
Ethereal
Weightless
Not scalding and visible
Not constant and pointless
Not at arm's reach when you should be sleeping
It should shudder out from your bones
It should press a pause in your thinking
Let you just be breathing
Just being
Some peace

That night
I sat down at his kitchen
For a moment I'd had time for a thought
'I'm being'
Not forced
Everything falls from my face
He smirks and calls it wisdom
But it feels more like a place
That I've been desperate to hold place in

Worked hard for money to have wasted
Trying to get there
Hours upon days, tapping, erasing
Flapping around in a haze
And calling it fashion
Calling it purpose
Calling it poetry
Calling it worse
Calling it escape
Calling it peace
When all it's been is piss paltry days
Of being stuck in modern ways

Not stupid, just learned
A manufactured calculated form
Of anxiety that is a dullness
Sizzling to fall and flatline as the norm
Beating myself up for not finding a way past it
So caught up in frustration that it's the only feeling
        that's lasting
Picking at pieces of the past begging them to be forecasting
But what has been and what isn't yours
Won't show you new
You can't simply expect peace in lieu
Of taking space to be it
Sometimes it takes waving surrender
Sitting down with kind eyes and with food
Sitting down with free hands
And to allow people to hold all of your weight
So there's a chance to make space inside of you
To allow people to hold all of your weight
Hold all of your being
So you can take it back again

And polish the peace that was always within you.

~Inspiring Quote on Backdrop of Ocean I'll Never Swim in~

I know we say
No pain no gain
But what I'm growing is a loss
Could it be a proverb unfinished
Or one with a last line that we forgot?

I know we say
No pain no gain
But is that what we really mean?
How about
No pain sounds nice
And gain is just for greed.

#instapoets

What's the point of having a good turn of phrase
When with it you've really got nothing to say.

The
Conception

All pink and flesh and naked
All screams and kicks and brazen
All hope and wide eyes, anticipating
Grabbing hands for mother's milk and smiling faces
All life and all love and all bundled up
Precious and gentle and soft to touch
All new, all you knew, was all them and no you
No thoughts only feelings, all life, all love.

And so they grow you with hope and with wisdom
They pick you up when you fall
And when you're wounded, they kiss them
They force feed you greens
And obsess on your teeth
Mild on minding your manners
And wild on watching you breathe
All that was once them is now you underneath
All body and bones, all genes
Prematurely bequeathed

But you grow and it falters
And you find an opinion
You rage and you range from
Your own person to minion
It happens and happens

It has done for years
But this time is different
New pressures, new fears
New notions, ideas
New things pressed in palms
That are born not of tradition
New measures for tears
New motions, pioneers and careers

New directions to choose
An invite to take pride to prize in a new exhibition
With everything you've not even owned yet to lose

You're pacified with sugar-free and a screen
You're shielded from truth but have access to obscene
You're cuddled and loved
Until it's time for TV
Join the table for adults
But quick! Here's your iPad!
Before you start to scream

You've got a phone with no numbers
But know all the buttons
Know your own rights
Before you know comeuppance
Not yet, not quite
It's about to hit you in waves
Micro-aggressions
Radio slaves
Ultra pressure
Visible early graves
Kiss chase is long gone
The adoration assumed
Why keep the parameter playground
When it can be publicly consumed?
Bios littered with Xs, dates, hearts all on file
Profess your innocence adult
Forget that you're still a child.

#notredamn

'I went there on my gap yaaah –
#blessed, My tears still stream.
Here's an essay on its beauty
Five photos vignetted on me.'
Silenced only to the notion
That we care less to protect the future
Than we do to rebuild history.

Emails From Elizabeth

My phone had been half-touched for days. Hands that used to jitter and shake, pocket grab and stroke, now sat upon, occasionally pulling at eyes, mostly reaching for a glass of wine; until now.

Of all my pathetic and medical addictions, the obvious glaring things that come with pictures of sick babies and bleeding gums printed on packets, this one that I swore was beneficial and not a benefactor to the others, has risen up to reveal all of its truths. I am drinking more and smoking more, my body is now coffee and debt, I blame it all on the devil and idle hands that are punishing my lack of swipe and simpering. I blame its toxicity for the others' latent lure – that I am carefully forgetting all came long before it. All my other crutches felt, through my phone, like lovely little brushstrokes on a caricature of me, this ludicrously dressed mad woman always offering out a lighter and smudging spilt wine with the other hand, phone safely nestled in bra ready to whip out to digitise it in all of its glory, a portrait of posterity.

But without it, albeit a few days and albeit notably lost because of a pulsating anxiety behind each eyelid and heavy in throat and throb of limbs, that portrait no longer hung. Its gilded frame is simply empty wall. Those things alone were dirty and sad and desperate. They needed, they were alive, on the anecdote and laughter, the tapped-in postcodes and lofty, last minute WhatsApp plans. The pirate red lipstick-stained bad habits could only be dragged out of bed in this state by friendship. By communication. Perhaps, much like the other things I hated to love, it was me that was the perpetrator, I was the problem. My need to constantly wash out silence instead of really listening to the whirring inner monologue of crapped-on cogs. Distraction. That's all any of this boiled down was. A magician blaming its faulty tricks when he himself had not mastered the magic at all. I was killing the doves before they had chance to fly.

The next evening, as I stopped to sit and write this in the grandeur of a bar I had screenshotted so many interior shots of it no longer felt exciting to actually sit in, I deleted the tweet.

I braved my email. Braved! What a hero! Who was this modern-day saviour, so stoic and nouveau?! Surely not I. But it was. A subject line glared through me and my eyes welled up in elation. It was Elizabeth.

Elizabeth who I'd met twice but, knew within a fraction of the first instance and consolidated on the second, knew me beyond the facade. She met me as me and liked me as this half-hashed idea of an adult that I was trying to grow into and to when I ran away from myself in body and mind. Here she was without a lifeboat, but an email to drag me ashore. A little rubber dingy-shaped offering filled with love and hope and reality (reality!), speeding towards me in the horizon. I'd mentally waved the white flag, brain just sparks of panic flare, I bloody well needed this days ago, I had received this days ago, but it was me who had denied it.

The doves started to flutter, all white and crisp and mesmeric, the dancing line that flashed and taunted after each new word that had legs to be absolution pulled at its chain, a new word, a new line, a new admission, a new honest recount of the dismal place my brain had reached, pulling pulling pulling, wings flapping and flapping and flapping until it felt such a cruelty to let them struggle any longer whilst they had such pure and powering intentions of freedom. So I let them. Before I shut off their wings back into my faulty box and lay furious that the words I needed had been waiting for me all along, the connection, the communion, I let them flap and fly to reply.

The back and forth, mammoth paragraphs of encouragement and update, lit me with all the things I had been hoping to find by running away and turning everything off. It dawned continuously, a buffering morning, that nearly everything that had happened, great and devastating, but with concentration on the great, had been possible because of the online world that I had grown up in and become so dependent on. Before my dependence, of which I was both to blame and a product of society, it had initially looked to me to be pearlescent gates that I owned the key to unlock whenever I needed to skip through and find something that I couldn't find anywhere else.

The nights at fourteen that turned into early mornings, making friends on forums discussing boys, and on many occasions saving strangers from the things that they couldn't bear to tell their parents or closest friends. The endless meme share and laughs and frankly incriminating WhatsApp messages that solved even the most intricate maladies. Photos found and reblogged that pushed me to believe perhaps one day I could take and one day did. Recipe blogs that proved to me cooking delicious meals was attainable, within my reach, good for my mind and my body. WikiHow that taught me, somewhat shockingly much later than I care to admit, you can in fact wee with a tampon in. WebMD that had convinced me of ailments that would later make them money, but also validate my symptoms that I couldn't articulate in real life and give me a second chance. The dating apps that joined me with heartbreak but also with now best friends of whom I know certainly I would not still be alive to write this without. The confidence that I had previously used it with, not a crutch, but as a tool, had shaped me to be the person sat alone in a bar five thousand miles from home, heartbroken and lost, sad and defeated, but with someone to pull me out and hope to keep me going. The former were things I was in control of and had lost hold of. The latter, a gift from the very thing that I had spent so long castigating that I could pick and choose the direction of but had held too firmly.

I flail from my bar stool and catwalk to the loo. I announce it to the suited waiter, 'Just popping to the loo!' and he laughs as I knew he would because they think it's charming and British and I know it's crass and uninteresting. It feels a half a step forward to acceptance. I am crass and uninteresting and somewhere deep down I love that, I hope.

The bathroom itself is incredibly opulent, the walls are coated in a flaked gold leaf and the mirrors have the sort of back light I would assume most 14 year olds now are able to fix to their front cameras. My eyes look tired, a bit drunk. But they upturn slightly as they survey each orange patch on my collar where my foundation has run from sweating and crying, sweating with anxiety of realisation, crying at the relief of just that. I tug at it and then laugh and then cry again and then sweat some more at the prospect of this very image existing on someone's CCTV footage. I half want to ask if I could get a copy, my brain whirring at what sort of Tracey Emin performance piece I could make this and then I stop.

I had placed my bag in the sink and had taken no caution as to think that a toilet as fancy as this one would likely have sensored taps. My bag filled with water and I just sort of watched it. I didn't flinch. After much, much too long, I picked out my belongings from the basin and smiled. Had I totally lost the plot? Or had I finally, like Andy in *The Devil Wears Prada*, thrown her phone into a Parisian fountain and realised I absolutely had the power to stop my life being so unbelievably miserable for the sake of appeasing a beast that the world worshipped but did me no good?

The transformation had been done. The portrait complete. I was an Anne Hathaway meme.

I, albeit totally penniless, albeit totally heartbroken, albeit five thousand miles from my actual home, had refound place and had taken back accountability. A product of all the things I thought so wrong had made me into enough of a person to turn them into riot acts of rights that I could now scream.

I don't want to have to say
'AM I RIGHT, LADIES?'
But

It is better to have loved and lost, than to never have loved at all. It is also better to resent something so passionately and then see it was just a mirror, than to have never owned a phone at all.

Am I right, ladies?

. . . answers please on the back of a postcard.

An Act in Six Parts

1.

'Is it a bit – upstage the bride?'
I spin in red chiffon
One trainer on, one heeled stride
Cinch in, pinch in, clinging to the sink's sides
'A bit yeah but step back in that light
No left
Left
Stand there, tilt your head right'
Think of the likes.

2.

Faces from a scene
Pulled straight from a dream
I can't believe I'm in
Kiss, hug, repeat to strangers with names
With followings to win.

3.

I am shiny at best
The charade feels convincing
Pushed and pulled from online
We stand shimmering, grinning
We all look like success
The emptiness hits
I am shiny at best.

4.

The open bar closes
My credit card's numb
So I leave, walk for hours
Put my trainers back on

I flick through the photos
Of the perfect night
Overwhelmed, close the app
Make a call, breathless fright.

5.
'Is it a bit – upstage the bride?'
I sit in red chiffon
One hand holding my wrist, the other rubbing my eye
Cinch in, pinch in, clinging to the ambulance side
'You made the right choice, drop embarrassment
Breathe
Is there anyone we should let know you came here before
        you leave?
This is only one night
Think of the rest of your life.'

6.
Nobody knows
They need not uncloak the glamour
Of a memory posted detailed enamoured
That beyond the parameters
Stepped outside of the screen
It was a bit upstage the bride
I tried to marry the end
When I was courting the dream.

#bodypositive

I like my body when I've eaten very little
I like my body when it's shared with other people
I like my body, not often, just sometimes
I like my body when my body isn't mine.

Objectify

Validate Me Part 1

Thought as much
Famed as such
Faked the touch
Of what excites us
Who we are and will always be
Unites us
But we seldom invite that side enough
Swapped it out to sell new love
As though it's not inside us

Think too much
Fame is such
A thing we'll fake as something that excites us
Spin it until we're spinning plates we can't dine off
Starving
Is this what we'll die of?
Vapid monsters in a sea of breeding nonsense, jealousy
Portraits of unfulfilled and pretty
Best lives or misery
Rooted to mis-sold faith in a downloaded commodity
Do you like me?
Do you like me?
I don't know who I am any more
I don't know who you are
Fascinate me as I fabricate me
Castigate me as I congratulate me
Salivate as I let you navigate me
Masturbate at how inadequate I find me
I'm putting it all out to see
No idea of what I want or who I am sans vanity
No idea of how to please our grumbling society
No idea of where I can slip off silently

I am halves with who I'm wholly miscalculating
Please, would you just validate me?

#candid

You only take photos when you think something might die
You only post photos hoping that it'll survive.

#fitspo

Smelling of fags and biscuits
Embers the colour of the bits that I missed.

The Party

The door opens quickly just as my earring falls out and breaks. Steph catches it and puts it in her pocket, seamlessly, and stares confidently at the man leaning and swaying on the frame. 'We're here for the party. Right house?' She says this with a vague tone of annoyance because it's bastard-freezing outside. Neither of us have tights on and he's just stood there gawping, assessing, working out if he'll get off with one of us by the dregs of the evening. Music crawls in muted tendrils down the tall staircase behind him. No bass.

'Well, hello girls. Who are you then?' An over-exaggerated mockney accent dribbles down his polo; when had people started to think that being mindful of your privilege meant performing a class act?

'This isn't Mahiki, mate. Let us in, would you?' It wasn't, thank God. It was a flat in Denmark Hill, with a door off to the back of a newsagents. Our legs are bare, shaking, and my mind clamours for space as it beats itself into a pulp wondering how I could've crammed another cigarette in-between the Uber and this unnecessary faux formality. 'Robbie invited us,' I say, meek in Steph's confidence, staring. I feel shiny. My face feels filled with obvious pores. I feel an intense fraudulence, which I'm sure is about to be exposed. I do not look like my photos. I am catfishing myself, at best. 'Course he did,' he stares at my boobs and Steph's legs. It feels almost like a compliment that neither of us would ever admit felt like one, we've spent enough time slagging off how Robbie always must be seen with the next hot girl and how he always has a line of them waiting, and how horribly disgusting and misogynistic that holds. But to be assumed to be one of them? An ego boost. 'So can we come in or what? Bloody hell.' This is boring.

'Yeah. Yeah, come up.' He steadies himself on the bannister and the noise of the party engulfs us as he swings open the kitchen door. Everyone stops for a moment.

'LADS! FOUND THESE TWO LOOKING FOR ROBBIE ON THE DOORSTEP,' he shouts with smackable smugness. Some roll their eyes whilst others cheer, others pay no attention at all and the girls move in closer to the men they're sat in front of.

'Drink?' Steph glares.

'Bathroom first. I'll sort out my face. Pour us one in there. Then let's give this a go.'

I hadn't been to a house party in years, the coy butterfly-sizzle of excitement about the hours of pre-game are lost and forgotten. Nothing about being stood in somebody else's bathroom with a cheap bottle of vodka between our legs felt naughty, it felt a bit grim and regressive. The fists banging on the door outside were not of rowdy teenagers who'd overdone it, not of new-found couples burrowing away for the night for a private snog, but of four thirty-year-olds after the cold, flat porcelain of the toilet to rack up lines of cocaine, which they'd later learn was actually ketamine. We let them bang.

'Remind me why we're here again?' Steph screws back on the cap of the vodka, wrestling with the cheap teeth on the cap that won't quite align. Impatient.

I ignore her, transfixed in my own reflection. I do not look like my photos and although I have spent countless lost, and wasted, hours studying the planes of my face to an almost scientific degree on my phone, it feels like the first time I'd really seen myself in months. Vulgar. Vile. I do not look like my photos. Of all the places to be incarcerated as a fraud, tonight's setting couldn't have been more perfect. As we'd walked flat-palmed, pushing doors in the dark to find the toilet, I had spotted five men I'd at some point matched with on Hinge or Bumble that had later gone on to ignore my witty, well-thought and, through a series of screenshots to friends, well-vetted opening lines. I had arrived at a place of uncloaking.

The banging becomes more incessant and grows to a kick that shoots the brass lock up and off its holder, the four men fall in crying with laughter, pulling each other down to pull themselves up in a twisted rugby scrum. I may not have looked like my pictures but they certainly didn't look like men. Little boys, still.

In the kitchen, it is much of the same tired scene we had left in the past of our pre-youth, where we were too young to be doing any of this at all but still stabbing at the perceived rituals of fun that we'd learned from films. Scattered plastic shells of shots and stepped-on crisps nestle deeper into the thin cracks of the wooden floor. No one here was having fun. Everyone is desperately ferrying around in a painted distraction, feigning merriment, if only to not feel cheated of the future they thought they'd be living for an hour or so. Thinking they'd have kids by now. A house. A holiday or two a year. A career. But here we were, acting fifteen, feeling forty-five, grappling for an artsy shot by the plugged-in disco lamp, rehashing unread articles that made one of us sound cultured and the other aggressive.

Empty.

Your Boyfriend in LA Loves Me From Across the Ocean

When was 'psycho' so sexy
Yet still castigated?
Everyone here is married
But they're all fucking, faking
When was dumbing it down
Cashing in as enough?
Who sold you the fear
That you need to be seen as in love?

They grin doe-eyed and warm
In every photo you post
Happy Valentine's, Babe
I Love You The Most
It all screens so perfect
But I scream DENIAL
Am I bitter and twisted?
Just crave a number to dial?

Scroll

Where are you finding these partners?
Will you teach me your rules?
What do you serve them for starters?

Are you drugging these fools?
How are they harnessed
So tight to your hip?

Bzzzzzzzzzzzz

Oh

A DM!
'I miss you gorgeous'
. . . sorry love, it's him.

Mercury in Retrograde

We are ruled by
A fool's literature
Our settled Sunday readings
Map out an astrology-pulled apology
For the curves and quirks in our hapless week's psychology

Clutching a passionate grasp around instruction
That limits our habits to the moon's and sun's seduction
We are led by the hand, willing participants in our
      own abduction
Lured by the romance of another world's aura –
      chunked construction

Running blind from our own control
Two thirsty dogs lapping from a cosmic bowl
Two sapient dogs lassoing a leash to their own soul
Dutifully bowing to boldly meditate
Around Leo's planetary heavyweights
Obediently howling at a weekly Mailchimp email to celebrate
A half-hashed understanding of Mercury retrograde

Cocking a leg to salute a sold faith
Doesn't the whole infinite eclectic point sort of dissipate
When we hand a stranger a title that lets them control our
      own fate?

'I Know I Can't Talk But . . .'

Darling
You and I are important
And what I thought to be suffering
Was an inkling and a drain
But what the world around you is doing
Is seldom progressive
Just shouting SAME
SHAME
SHAME
Never looking back at the woman
Who was privileged enough to realise
Those sentiments were a gain.

#whatafeministlookslike

Dyed of its natural conditions
Died of its misconvictions.

Aesthetic

The glamour is better
When you're less put together
It's real it is felt
It's authentic
All that you are and all you exude
Weighs out its aesthetic.

Self Care

There is only a trace of anaesthetic
In the aesthetics
There is no truth, no freedom
No Holy Spirit's leading
In the clang of rose-gold copper self care
There is only growth in muddled despair
There is help in the hurting
In the muddied soul searching
In pulling it all out of mind for your eyes to see
It's mad – a cruel charade
For anyone to sell back your sanity
In bubble baths
Face masks
And breakfast in a bowl from Anthropologie.

The Walk-in Centre

Looking around, brush strokes of broad bored glances, everyone looks perfectly healthy. A little ruddy-cheeked from the December air and a faint suggestion of office-party regret, but no one looks like they are dying. Not that I know what the early stages of dying look like, but there is a disappointing lack of green gills, limbs hanging off, and intestines snaking the floor like stomped-on internal telephone wires. I suppose they think the same of me. Able-bodied, aggressively highlighted cheeks, bags of late Christmas shopping (the Urban Outfitters sale starts on the 20th so why bother buying all your crap prior?) and a fake limp so bad that I catch eyes with one man who gifts me a gentle ticklish cough, pulling it from his throat in solidarity, and we both do an awkward inward laugh. Ah, communion.

There is a lump on the back of my knee, which WebMD suggests is likely to be stage IV cancer or a golfing injury. I don't play golf. I am clearly dying. I wonder if everyone else here has convinced themselves that they are dying too? WebMD has become a form of idle procrastination for me, sometimes even when I am perfectly fine I'll click the parts of the digitised body and input symptoms just to see what they amount to. If they have any correlation. I am certain now that any time when I feel an organ fizz, I've got a spot on my right cheek or my ankles click, I can do some sort of WebMD-informed maths to convince myself I have a terminal illness. There is something about finding logical, even though it's not, impermanence to life that soothes my anxiety. There is something about finding pattern and reasoning in my body's shortcomings, and potential failings, that makes the notion of a suicidal thought seem quite quaint when I can convince myself my body is ready to give up before I give it permission to.

Not that long ago mental illness, albeit taboo and often dismissed even when as real and as profound as someone with suicidal ideation – there was a certain sympathetic coup for it. An arm rub. A waft of misunderstanding that means it is serious. Yes, it was saved for nutters and mad women, but it was also serious. There were institutes. Slurs. But now it just feels assumed. I don't feel any new communion with the movement of celebrities 'admitting' their anxiety and depression, I feel annoyed. I feel 'fuck'. There's already next-to-no resource, what happens now more people use it? It also feels a bit self-aggrandising. This idea of admitting.

The hero worship that would come off the back of it. I hate it. In a world so saturated for content, this feels like the new obvious like-worthy filler. Draw it out on an Obama-style YES WE CAN poster and it could be 2008 again. My illness isn't Kony. So fuck off. Depression and anxiety feels cancerous to me, but it no longer sounds like a killer. We've all got it. We're all being sold it in a breath of good deed and a lack of education. In fact, it's not different to how it once was. We still know nothing, the pharmaceutical companies are rubbing their hands, and we're all still mad and not being taken seriously. Only now everyone's being mis-sold their mental health, the thing we've all got and all must look after, as though it's an illness. As though we're all broken. As though any quirk or human emotion is a defect. So sometimes I like to convince myself there's something more physical, more appalling sounding, more known, so I can get a week off. Or a life off. So I can explain my struggles to an apparently new woke world in a way that gets some proper sympathy instead of a #MeToo. It sounds awful I know, but sat in this surgery, staring down faces who also don't look like death, I apply the 1-in-5 statistic and realise at least ten of us are here because of our brains. Ten. And I'm here saying it's cancer because my real killer doesn't feel real and I wonder who else is doing the same. I daren't say it to anyone ever because I sound worse than a climate change denier. I sound ungrateful. But in a realm of fake news and sold thought, that feels about as radical and free as I can think. How sad.

I shuffle about once my name's been called, ferrying heavy bags and a comedy limp to greet the doctor.

'I know! I know! I'm coming in with a leg problem and here I am with all these heavy bags like I can handle it!' I'm lying, apologetic, and unable to hear the echoing irony that will ring once she's read my medical records and knows how to properly understand them, if she can.

'Take a seat, love. I'll ask you a few questions and then I'll have a feel to see what's the matter.'

A feel to see what's the matter. Brilliant. Unzip me from the ears and watch like ticker tape as it falls, celebratory around my knee lump. Therein lies the problem!

She transforms from doctor to mouse, sheepishly suggesting that I have a womb.

'I have to ask this to all females, sorry – is there any possibility of you being pregnant?'

I love that she must disclose this as a run-of-the-mill question, as though once a woman walked in and complained to someone that they thought she was an easy whore who had unprotected sex, and was deduced as such from sitting in front of her GP.

'I bloody hope not.'

In-between

Protruding
From both brain and skin
Seeping hungered odour
Someone please comment
'She's so thin!'
I want the worry now
I want anxious stares
Dreaming up
What once was there
I no longer want to be a half
One meal sounds plenty
I'll only ever make it
When my body meets my mind

And they feel the same: empty
I won't say it
It's not progressive
But it's streaming in aggressive
With every post
I am rewarded for being confessive
But my honesty now feels like boasts
They don't sound worrying
My body though not deemed extreme
Too small to warrant pressure
Too big to feel so mean
Wrecks itself unseen
In a sea of good-willed positives
Why do I now feel too in-between?

The internet is a horrid fickle beast. For the first half of my career I was bullied for being 'fat'. As soon as I opened up about feeling that way I was told I wasn't big enough to feel what they'd castigated me for.

Snakes

You spit and you spit
Until there is no more
Ankles bound in venom
Piles of your innards bile
Across the floor
You never knew the fool that you'd become
The sort to be bitten by riposte
And for it to have sunk in and almost won.

Tubes

I fumble for my headphones
Snakes amidst the mess
My fingers untangle, furiously
As you shake your head

It swings, a nod come gesture
You jitter with your hands
You smile and look straight through my soul
I move rings to suggest I have a man

Music 'on', the signal's gone
I tap my feet to what I can't hear
The safety of knowing you won't say
'You alright, darlin'?'
Because there's white plastic in my ear.

Bad Feminist

I need to feel sexy
I need to be strong
I need to be assertive
In my right to be wrong
I'm confused, I've got lost
Am I the woman that I wanted?
Am I hashing out ideals
All excuses – fair of plaudit

Do I shout the loudest?
Were these things I had on a list
That my womanness was afraid to profess
Because I felt they couldn't coexist
Or
Have I passified myself
By defining my integrity
As believing that every thought I own
Is nothing more than internalised misogyny?

I've been angry
              I've strangled fear
I've beaten at the ceiling
                          I've pulled quotes and statistics near

I've fought, I've yelled, I've felt
I've demanded
I've tried to help

But sometimes it all just feels imported
Is this my truest self
Or am I just a man-pleasing woman
Exhausted?

#spon

It used to be tits
Nestled in headlines
A break from the crude?
Flip to page 3, check out the nude
It used to be lips
Sucking on Flakes
Want a dose of arousal?
Skip to the ad breaks
It used to be legs
On bonnets of cars
She'd only be seen
On the right arm
It used to be trashy
Demeaning and brutal
It all seemed so brazen
So obvious, so futile
We gained it all back
I felt so empowered
Until I realised sex still sells
But this time to me:
Young girls –
Vitamins and whey powder
Clothes that don't fit
On the bodies they sit
Cinched in and smoothed
Hungry eye glares removed
Just sexy
And tiny
Sexy and tiny
Soft, lithe and shiny.

Validate Me Part 2

So dreamless now that is all that is left
What and who and why to be
When nothing but the truth is far-fetched
How to feel when it all seems in reach
A dangling carrot stick of a life
With only The Cloud(s) underneath

Where to begin and how to see
Why to feel and who to be
What promises to land
What honesty laid bare to keep
A dangling carrot stick of a life
With limited data to glean

So dreamless and chaotic
In the best way
Leading the oppressed day
Into one that is knowledge
Trying to feed off the same grown
That everyone else has new forged
When did the pandemic become organic?
Why am I in a panic?
Goodness was once transparent
Not an assumed apparent
If not given in abundance

Cancelled! Finished! Abhorrent!

So dreamless now that is all that is left
So schemeless, yet that was once my success
So diminished in that goodness to invest
Frittered it away to an account with no salvageable interest

Nothing means less than what I detest
Try to confess
What I have left
So please please just
Validate me
I'm confused, I'm bereft
It's all I have left
This exhaustion, frank and spent
It's all I have left
So please please just
Validate me.

Love

Acceptance Is the First Step

My neck creaks and crunches in unison with the seemingly unending pop and ping of the notifications blurting from my phone. There is a microwave pun in there somewhere, but the second bottle of wine between me and my girlfriend assures that we won't find it on the tips of our tongues. Just more wine. We 'deserve' it. Or I do, specifically. She comforts me – reminding me that despite my relationship woes, the confusion and conflict of having to announce having a 'not-boyfriend', a man whom in every conventional sense is my boyfriend (he's stuck around for breakfast after spending the night at mine for four months for Christ's sake, as though that is a real status and one that I am complicit with), I can still behave as though I am a carefree singleton. It pops, it pings, again, again, an Instagram vibrate, a Tinder nudge.

Creak, crunch, pop, ping.

'Trying to keep eye contact with you is like attempting to stare at the horizon on the fucking Titanic, babe.'

I blame it on the new pillow I've been using. It's a bloody expensive one; but I didn't have to pay for it. A hashtag footed the bill. I cling to the brand partnership in conversation like a 90s pop star thrusting their first newspaper pap photo at a mate to show they're making it. To prove their career is setting off. To show they've got some kind of vague but tangible place in pop culture. My worth as a person, a writer. A free pillow.

'Just because it's free, doesn't mean you have to sleep with it.'

We both laugh. Wine. Perhaps too much.

'I've told people it's like an angel's bosom caressing my shoulder blades, I can't back out now, I'm building myself on authenticity. I am suffering for my art AND my money.'

I raise my glass and then roll my eyes back in disdain. I hate myself. The pillow is like an angel's bosom, right? I've probably just strained a muscle from five years of carrying my laptop in my handbag and sleeping on friends' sofas. How many pillows will it take to make rent?

She contorts her body to bend back on her chair and forces a double chin with elbows next to her ears to get a candid photo of me looking fine and happy in the restaurant we can't afford. The waiters are rude, the food is small, the other diners are thin and boring but there's a Shrigley painting behind my head and the bathrooms have rose-gold taps and exposed tile floors that will survive a season or two more.

I slide the two empty bottles of wine out of eyeshot. Drinking is bad for you. Did you know that more than a quarter of millennials don't drink? Bad for your brand. I reach for a cigarette.

Creak, crunch, pop, ping.

The night before, propped up in bed with the pillow, face aglow with the muted night-mode light, I realised I was going mad. I text several friends to let them know – a new WhatsApp group of my favoured, most-trusted women – a message littered with enough siren emojis to suggest a family death. 'One of you needs to take me out tomorrow night. It's URGENT.'

I was going *mad* and it was not my usual flavour of neurological illness, not my usual predisposed millennial anxiety nor a *bona fide* disorder. This was a downloaded, delusional madness. For the love of fuck, the one thing I'd promised myself I wouldn't let happen was happening and filtering through my body with each exposing swipe.

I had gifted myself a personal agreement in the midst of the good times, pre-empting the inevitable end (it is seemingly always inevitable), that I wouldn't become another one of those 'crazed bitches', the ones my father and ex-boyfriends spoke of. The ones so steeped in paranoia, doubt and fear that their wiring would jump start at the flash of a screen. They'd scream and slap and stomp about. They'd post passive-aggressive Facebook statuses, issue out thirst-trap photos across all platforms. They'd make a scene.

As I lay in bed next to my 'not-boyfriend', his arms wrapped tight around me as I slid my forefinger over my phone, I felt my character change. I was becoming Her. I tried to breathe through my nose, clench my thumbs, meditate to cherish the moment of being held, reinforce the feeling that one day I'd look back on this and miss it. But truly I wanted nothing more than to suffocate him with the pillow and march out with my hands on my head shouting: 'I know about the other women! I know you don't love me! And I know you think I'm fat and you cringe when I speak! And-and-and-I know that you're still on that app.'

I didn't know any of these things, not really. Not a single one. But I had my dwindling self-esteem and fervent state of paranoia to form a stealthy hunch. He owned a phone, it was all perfectly possible and all incredibly likely. I was wrecked and there it was. Laid bare. I had become the woman, the irrational psychopath, the sort of girl that a guy gets black-out drunk in front of the football to forget about.

Worse still, I was internally describing myself as such, I'd become the perfect portrait of the awful misogynistic paintings that the seemingly endless stream of fuckboys had sold to me as unreasonable and unattractive, and I was selling myself off to the gallery, pricing myself up to the patriarchy, banging nails in the wall to be hung willingly.

'Go on! Marvel at my emotional craze! Am I on my period? No. But my fertility app says PMS is likely right now, so IMAGINE WHAT I'LL BE ABLE TO AUCTION NEXT WEEK.'

Not even my half-hearted, I'll-turn-up-to-a-Trump-march-for-a-well-intentioned-placard-pose feminism wanted to interject. I was actually Her. Jesus, how do you hate yourself these days without offending yourself?

Politically exhausted, personally bereft, physically poised to pounce at sending 80 generic 'Hey, cool profile. Fancy a drink?' slurs across the dating apps I'd deleted weeks prior. But I saved my data and text the girls instead.

Bursting from the seams, an almost masochistic euphoria – a failed lover, a failed feminist, a failed brand ambassador – no longer conforming to the internet's ideals, good or bad. It took a mere four and a half minutes until I was back on my phone scrolling an endless cycle, whimpering for validation. I am code-dependent and consumed, longing to just be liked, pushing off the arms of real validation into the grips of repetitive strain disorder.

Creak, crunch, pop, ping.

Score

I won't stand for being tested
I am not a pupil
I am a friend, a lover
And even if you are testing upon which one of those I am
Test yourself
Don't text me.

Downloveable

You're always a Sunday
Even one I dread
But waking up on Monday
I'm not dead
And that's you
You're the realisation
Left on read
You're the tangible hope of life
You're the frustration of feeling so alive

You're the love I need
That I thought you'd denied
Until I stopped, sat in present
To see it was mine to decide

You're the love I need
That I thought you'd denied
But something so large, so overflowing
Can't be hinged on a reply

You were all the love I needed
That I chose to deny
When I was scared it was mine.

'Can a Machine Understand the Human Heart?'

I've googled in the future
I scroll back throughout your past
I live within a moment
Where I thought that this might last
I've read up on our horoscopes
Checked what your sex moves mean
But my heart's still in your bed
My head's still in your sheets
Where I counted seconds of your breath
That you snored across my nose
I still feel your legs
Seeking warmth from mine as opposed
To the heat you warmed yourself with
The fired confidence I'd never known
I shrunk to be a body
Not your fault, maybe his
Now no search word, stars aligned
Can make sense of feeling this
Can a machine understand the human heart?
What difference does it make
When clearly we both can't?

Push Notifications

Happy birthday
I don't mean it
I hope it's awful
An empty bar
Because all your friends were on holiday
Happy birthday
I don't mean it
I hope your parents got confused
And text your sister instead
Happy birthday
I don't mean it
I hope you're filled with dread
That I got a push notification
To remind me you weren't dead
And I wished you were.

141

I called your old landline on withheld
Just in case
Just to see if everything had changed
Four years later
I woke up your mother
The number was the same
And she drew a panicked breath
And sober-sleep-spoke HELLO?
You used to tell me I was insane
I lay the phone beside my head, turning up the volume
HELLO? . . . HELLO?
I hear her impatience, footsteps crashing to crescendo
She swings on a door
Tired eyes audibly dragging on the floor
IT MUST BE FOR YOU, THEY WON'T SPEAK TO ME
My body rattled
My ears pricked
Heart still settled
Until
'What . . . why for me?'
HELLO?
HELLO?
It was you
I never had any intention of speaking

There were no questions keeping
Me awake
I just wanted to see if everything had changed
And I can only assume it hasn't
Midnight and you are not in bed
Midnight and we've hung up before things were said
Remember when we thought we could be in love?
Midnight I still call as secret

I will take this midnight slice
In its oddity and keep it.
Worlds apart yet still connected
If only when I called your mobile
You'd accept it.

Modern Love

Was it written for us
Before we unmasked its disguises?
Was it planned and then pieced apart
So we would build machines to find it?
Was it always there
Unbothered by missed encounters
Sitting sweet and patient
Whilst we text into the early hours?
Was it always this much admin?
Devoid of purity
What was love
Before you swiped right for me?

Born of Hope

Much like a parents' time

The best we had was before we could speak

Much like a parents' time
The most magical was before we knew each other, had picked
out names
But we didn't know how it would sound when we spoke our
first words
Despite the expectation
Notification kicks
Feeding my life thinking it would seep down umbilical to
make you fatter with me
I'd sing to you down a text like it would make you smarter

Pieces of me and the father too, pieces of anticipation
But you were born not mine.

A surrogate to hope and a mother to loss
Snatched on your final term
Given to someone more experienced
Much like a parent's time
The burnings of joy in the conception
The yearning for more physical communication
The praying for unconditional validation
The swings of highs and nervous lows, the wait of months,
all nine
The irony not one bit lost

Booty Call

My hand sits flaccid in my lap
Limp with guilt that it's betrayed me
Conscious of the grip it stole
Lifted, to attention, obeying
A command I didn't give it
A force all of its own
It rose with such excitement

Before it knew what it was saying
The repercussion is a buzz
It's dangerous
Exciting
Until it falls between my legs
To shine what it's inviting

It's all so fleeting, but I feel shamed
I'm drunk and I know better
The truth is nothing
Conscience weak
My limbs have their own vendetta

It's still aglow
Dropped on the floor
A fool
A slut
I'm dumb
I should've known from the beginning
It would've taken more for him to come.

Discover Page

I wander, wonder, walk for hours
Procrastinate
Forget the running water, cold shower
From sat to hunched to on my back
Feet in the air, nonplussed to sad
It stops me in my untraced tracks
Index poised, a gentle tap
There she is, a face I know
Burning me through a cold glow
A name I've written in my mind
Yours there too, indelibly signed
You're no longer mine
I've seen what you refuse to say
You're no longer mine.

#bestself

I don't want to be you anymore
Syncopated heartbeats
Throat tied up tight and dragged across the floor
I've been studying myself for days
Staring down
An entire ache
Life dulled to eye sores
I don't want to be you anymore
Whoever whatever why ever she is
I've been studying my ways
Sifting through their online archive
I haven't seen myself for days.

Overseas

It's mad where they'll bring you
It's mad where you'll go
Offshore with no confidence
Just entirely alone
5000 miles from home
I'm documenting it so you will see
A pointless performative charade
When for the first time in months
We're sharing the same city
It's mad what you do
Strung up in a toneless assumption:
That if you throw yourself out there
Really live with some gumption
That the words that you thought were
All laid out in blue shapes
Could read as a compass
Pulling towards a new space

It's mad when you get there
And it all ends so swiftly
Just a ten-minute phone call
Spluttered, selfish and sickly
That the power of what's in your hands
Is not the device nor that of a man's.

It's how you pick yourself up
And reassess this strange place
To know you still own your own map
And perhaps this is fate.

Fresh in the realisation I'd attempted to move to LA for a man who didn't love me — I wrote this in my friends, Will and Arden. front garden in Venice. It was the first thing I'd been able to write for weeks

Elvis

He warned us of the fools who fell
But where is the wisdom to the persistent
To those who've ritualised their morning thoughts
To eighty new men
Their Singha beer tank tops
And David Attenborough dream dinner guests
Looking for nothing too serious
No one who takes themselves that way
Someone to listen to the time in Thailand
They got caught up in a cartel
Had their lives changed for the better, anyway
He warned us of the fools who fell
But where is the wisdom for the downloaded
Demanded, diligent, demeaned love dreamers who stumble
Nobody could croon it, no compassion possible
I wish Elvis had lived to see Bumble.

Obsessed

Last seen:
9:16
Wake up,
Stop sleeping
And forgetting about me.

'Typing . . .'

Hovered,   hesitant
The thin line flashes
I exhaust the   pause
Until it's silent no more

And you are forced to expel everything you mean.

Glowing

When you wake your eyes are drawn to the screen
And I imagine all the people before us
Who didn't have these things
Who'd have lazed and lounged and gazed
Touched and smiled and yawned and snaked
I don't need your hand in the street
I don't need our parents to meet
I don't need *6 months* as a feat
I just want to know that all that's between us
Beneath the sheets
Is your eyes and mine
Our legs intertwined

Instead of waking up to you on your sodding phone.

Fake Muse

I matched with a model
Surely it can't be
What on earth would a model
Ever see in me?
He asked me out for dinner
Suggested we met at his
Turned out he was actually 56
5ft 4 with 3 kids.

#girlboss

Why does a prefix
Equal characters, equal weight
Become the thing that stirs and shakes
Boss would be enough
If we were just fucking paid the same.

The Break-up

No sentiments sweet nor sour enough, no explanation worthy, no justification, no justice. As I woke to smugly catch my alarm before it had set off, a text had already set in. The months of wondering when we would both finally commit, take the grand leap of faith to monogamy, of which whilst I told myself I had already arrived at, knew truly, my digital actions spoke otherwise – over.

I had always thought myself a connoisseur of heartbreak, so very good at feeling melancholy and victimised, so very talented at believing I was born from a line of princesses trapped in towers with no saviour but alas, no more. I was strangled in fear, smothered by the truth. All that I had put off now emboldened in front of me with a back light. It wasn't what was said, the punctuation was not in the phrasing nor in the truths, it was how it had been delivered. A text.

The cowardice stung and raged through my body, ravaging away at each synapse that once heated to glow potential and future and fondness, now sizzling to rage. Occasionally cooling to anguish. I put my phone back under my pillow and sobbed, salty strings of wet and snot.

I had enjoyed living in a wistful denial, I had become so comfortable and freed in its endless confines of performance work and Cheshire grins and having someone to talk about casually in conversation. The significant lack of pressure from having a significantly silhouetted significant other, I relished in excusing all of the unhealthy and damaging lacking pieces because at least, in anecdote, they were still present pieces. Month upon month of carefully spinning my own web of comfort around the eight-legged beast of truth, not in malice or for love of deception, but so desperately caught up in feeling the validation of being seen to be in love. Of kidding myself my worth amounted to being of worth to someone else, and being of worth to others too. I knew, too, that no sympathy would come of this, and why should it? I had willingly and knowingly put myself here deep within an expanse that at some point had to start closing in.

These feelings, whilst felt but so perpetuated and manufactured, had to eventually learn their own language to scream back asking not to be abused any longer. A fool's game. I had birthed a Frankensteinian form of love and the bolts that kept its head together were unscrewing themselves. This was not a heartbreak that I knew how to deal with nor how to process, it was such deep shame and mortification. It, like the goodness I thought pervaded, took hold of my sanity.

Eventually, I got out of bed, I got myself here. Stood on the platform.

It terrifies me, resolutely, every time I see it. What if it just buffers me off? What if I'm not quick enough? What if I catch the driver's stare and change my mind and only get my ankle decapitated? What if I can't kill myself properly. A failure at killing myself. They'd love that.

'She couldn't even get that right.' Slap it on a list under tax returns and cooking rice, uploading at the optimum audience retention time and replying to anyone, ever. My inner rhetoric still so skewed to speak and perform to others even when it was pushing at itself. Nobody could read my mind here, nobody cared. It ranted in thirty different voices as to how my end would be perceived if it even happened.

I let it go on and on until it was hoarse, exhausted, until it felt different. All of the wild sparking mental chatter and doubt sparking until it was gone, everything just still. I stood in it. Breathe in for eight, hold for eight, breathe out. Nonplussed in the gust of hot Bakerloo Line air making hard acquaintance with the headlights in my mind's eye. I felt nothing at all. Just present. I forgot for all of six fleeting, flashing seconds, everything. In this moment I was just a really terribly sad person, an inconvenience to commuters, that was clutching at the tip of a final straw sitting in cyanide. Feeling present was only an inch easier than feeling like someone who cased together all of those thoughts.

I got out when I could bear signalless distraction no longer and walked to a corner shop at the end of a road I could only identify as a place I'd once seen bleary-eyed at an off hour of the morning leaving a man's house after predictable and sloppy drunk one-time sex. I smirked. I wondered if I got a map of London and scribbled all the streets I'd only ever been to once for regrettable encounters if it'd make a fun artefact for future older me to reference when I was missing my youth. I smirked again. Jesus, I was nearly smiling. Wriggling around in the gentle and genuine hilarity of making fun things for future me when I had zero intention of lasting the next four hours.

'Twenty b&h blues and that delicious looking bottle of tequila please.' Surely no one could be miserable when sipping from a tiny plastic novelty sombrero. Life science. Surely.

'How old are you?' the man behind the counter grumbled, hardly turning his head from the small portable TV he'd made little effort to conceal in an old crisp box. It was barking out broken sound bites of Takeshi's Castle. How the fuck had he managed to find a channel still showing it? Impressive. I decided I liked him.

'Twenty-three in four days.'

He swivelled round fully to assess the facts. A quick once over, up and down eyes that stopped efficiently at my cleavage.

'Lucky you.' he said, no smile.

I liked him no longer. 'Lucky?' Pah!

'I remember that age. Celebrating nothing but all the time.'

I'd passed without even fingering for my provisional licence. He gifted me my official title as an adult and then placed my other equally-as-important incidentals into a Colgate striped bag, nodded his head as the satisfying beep of the contactless payment authorising rung through to release me.

'Have a really lovely evening.' I didn't care about his evening much at all but it helped with the charade. I had got very good at being a convincing shadow of a happy, put-together person through being aggressively polite to my core. He'd already turned back to his screen, safe in the knowledge that I wasn't the sort of person to be skulking underground considering my meagre life options. I was a 'lucky' young girl with a plastic bag of tricks and fun with a whole Friday night ahead of me. What could there possibly be to worry about?

'Where are you?' Thirty texts blimped in. Almost all of them question marks. 'Helloooo??'

'Ok I'm getting worried now.'

'Why is your phone off?'

'Wait, have you blocked me?'

Hazed, I slumped against the wall of the shop, I was just staring, not really reading. He continued to type.

'OH THANK GOD, they've gone through. Sorry. I thought you'd died or something lol.'

There had been many, many points in our non-relationship where 'lol' had frustrated me to a point of lobbing my phone from one side of my bedroom to the other, screaming muffled into my white knuckled fists. Lol, simply put, was the death of us. Lol, more poignantly put, was the disconnect and crack in conversation which he'd chisel every time I wanted to talk about anything that warranted more emotional lineage than the meme he was hell bent on picking apart. Three letters, taunting, the most inane piece of punctuation. How do you reply to lol? How do you come back from it? You don't. Lol is where lots of love comes to die and, in turn, almost me.

Another text, pushing me to the ends. I wanted to call him, fall to my knees and scream, 'You BRUTE. You've done this. How could you possibly end all of this over a text? Is that all I was? Nine months! A text! Done! Over!' but soon realised, with a few words rearranged, a few time stamps altered, that was exactly what I should've been shouting at myself.

#woke

I woke up this morning
Misinterpreted my privilege
I'll tell you I'm mourning.

Suffocate

Selfish Care

My will-he-won't-he relationship had been officially he-won't for a few weeks and in-between convincing myself I was dying of terminal illness, loathing the bones of my body, and incurring incredibly impressive debt to Deliveroo and Klarna, it was the sight of his name that churned my insides in the most cruel and undignified way. I had been avoiding department stores (and now, even my beloved Duty Free) in terror: one stray squirt of his aftershave could kick the backs of my knees in and have a pristine woman from behind the beauty counter calling security, gagging me with her silk neckerchief as I smash each bottle off the shelf like a T-Rex who'd finally afforded his arm extension op.

'A sample, Madam?'

'A sample of nauseatingly happy times? Get stuffed, mate.' I couldn't risk it.

But the other places lingered under my nose still, the other places not only unavoidable but greeting me with every waking second as though they were doing me a kindness. 'Suggested' lists, unopened voicemails, photos begging to have the faces recognised, filling my body with the most putrid acid, concocting another cocktail in my stomach. So far down in the pit of my intestines it was almost comically a shooting pain in my rectum. Anxiety, leading the way to remind me of what he really was.

The melodrama of my every thought and sense had pursued me to Heathrow, one 11-hour flight away from freedom of heart. It had chased me down with such aggression that asylum was all I had left. The notion of feeling so uncomfortable and rigid had become a certain kind of comfortable – one that I was frightened to keep seeking comfort in. Perhaps, I thought, if I unleashed myself to the swell of spontaneity, just like all other good bourgeois heroes of mine whose stories I'd dogeared and underlined and idolised, perhaps if I forced myself to truly just ~live~, I would be able to recapture a sanity so long ago felt. I can hardly help myself as I walk through the connecting flight tunnel and before I turn my phone off I hit send on a tweet that simply says 'Goodbye, strange world.'

'Good.' I think. 'Ambiguous.' I think. 'My friends might worry, strangers might offer sympathy.' I think. 'This buys me some time, to see if anyone really, truly, actually cares.'

Flight mode on.

It's selfish and it reeks, but no more than the man who sits himself behind me and reclines his seat barefoot and rests a toe on the arm of my chair, I reason, half convinced. I suppose when given the opportunity to do as we please and block out the immediate consequence, we are all the same.

I unpack my kit meticulously. Oils and self-heating eye masks, miniscule sample pots that have been labelled with numbers to ensure they are slapped on in the right order. One book on leadership (I have never worked in an office), a copy of *Letters of Ted Hughes* (it is almost the weight of my check-in luggage and I, for the most part, hate Ted Hughes), a notebook (laden with past haunting memories best left unchecked up on and with few pages left to make any real new notes) and my laptop (of which I have idly forgotten to charge enough to watch all three series of The Durrells). I wish so desperately I had a to-share bag of chocolate buttons, a Sally Rooney and some cheap make-up wipes. The young woman next to me eyes it all up, salivating from Drunk Elephant to Chantecaille, head cocked at Parker pen and Google Pixelbook, opening her mouth at Ted –

'That's quite an impressive spread you've got going on – you're, like, professional at long haul.'

I smile, accomplished. She asks to take a photo of it, accomplishment.

Ferrying back and forth from the toilet at a great rate of knots, there are so many damned steps to kidding myself that this is a well-earned indulgence, I have wasted three hours and missed the food trolley twice by the time I've ripped the perforated line of lavender sleep aid, but it has caught the eyes of several other female passengers, all stopping when they do eventually catch me in the line for the loo (again), to ask what hyaluronic acid I use. I don't, but I mutter something about The Ordinary over Glossier with cool nonchalance and trudge back to my seat much more disgruntled dervish at the thought of having to get up to wipe whatever heavy muck I've just slicked under my eyes and left all over the sink during turbulence than serene wafting angel of essential oil and inner clarity and calm. I am kidding myself of total connoisseur-ship; it feels so good, all velvety and lux, the idea that other women value my opinion without knowing an ounce of what sits behind my silk sleep mask. It has all risen to a perfect and intricate soufflé of me perhaps being the lost daughter of an Eve Babitz-type on her way to storm Beverly Hills. In an instant I can imagine the wealthy old men I plan to prop myself up on a barside with, the old-fashioned way, to humour and engage with and, as my great-grandmother once joked, leave a banana peel out for once we had inevitably got married much to society's shame and mockery. I could even see my own reflection in my black patent Louboutins, wiping a single solitary tear that miraculously leaves no mascara, clutching a silk pocket square that he owned well before I was born. What a farce. I take half a Propranolol when I think about how much it all cost, forcing me into a haze of whisky, comatose. It turns out all I needed to relax was, in fact, my medication.

I think a lot about whether or not anyone will have seen my tweet yet. What time is it at home and did anyone remember I was leaving? Those who don't know me, do they think I've died? I hope they don't, I truly hope they don't, but there is a sprinkling of sociopath fizzing deep down inside of me – someone that once started off moderately concerned with content curation –

that is rocketing against the walls of my soul waiting to full-on Berocca effervesce into that kind of arsehole. Shit, maybe I already was. Shit, why on earth was this even a thought that I could begin to simplify, justify, in my head? How had I made up the face and the mind of someone who I was so far from with the organs and failings of someone I'd always been? When had I let the meshed veil enmesh into me? Whose funeral was I excited to wipe tears at?

I Am Too Many Characters For This

When I wanted anything at all
But no one felt familiar
Or safe
Strangers felt the place

My teeth hurt from biting
A dull pulse

Close eyes
Drip

Drip

No one is awake to alert
I would not wake anyone to this state

Frightened

Absolutely fucking terrified

Close eyes

Drip

Bite

Are you awake?

No response
My last message can't be a tweet

My last words can't be public

But in the end

They would be anyway

As a warning

Close eyes

Drip.

4feiting Grandad

1.

The ghosts that you see
Are me
Always at your foot
Crumpling the bed covers
Telling you what's for tea
As soon as
We can both swallow again

New-found cuts
So long hidden
Prick and sting
Smothered in silken anti-bac
Tiny slits that scream
I would endure a thousand more
To be sure that you'll come back

2.

Gulping down diluted bitter lemon
We trace your gravy lips with paper
Your good hand squeezes, your bad hand holds
Us holding back on things you couldn't make
For what we'd give to take this all away
You think in new voices and speak the language you could save
Your good hand tickles, your bad hand holds
Out for connection in the days
The only thread you seem to pull
Is that when we're together things can pause
To sit and know
To sit and show
Memory-scapes of feelings will always light and love the same

3.
Last Christmas I sat face deep in a text
Fearful of what our next interaction would be
And you laughed
And noticed
And I'm so angry I was so cowardly
And pushed away from asking you all the questions about
     everything
And nestled into screen

And now
Every time I see the picture of us as my screensaver
I can't hear you laugh

I want to scream

4.
The magic
So pure and undiluted
Of your laugh
The half
Of your smile
The prickle of the wry upturning
Of a presence unpresented for a while
The melted chocolate and Zovirax
Twisted on my finger
As I prod at lips and teeth
To feel a shape that had always been there
Just unprovoked

Four hours have passed
Time full with purpose and belonging
I haven't once looked at my phone.

Comparison

How did she get so beautiful
So struck with all the sharpest planes?
I'm stuck down in a lasting pain
What I would give
I wouldn't eat
To have that face, even her feet
Can't stand the sight of toes
But I'd pull mine off just for her nose
None of this is love
Not infatuation
Just sad self-degradation
I'd take it all and never give it back
Wear it like the only skin I've ever had
How did she get so beautiful?

How did I get this mad?

Convenience

It's a blessing!
What a miracle to be bestowed
Thai food and taxis
All straight from my phone!
How did I live before
Endless freedom and curry?
Oh right, of course
I used to have money.

Silent

What's winning about worry?
I just want silence to stand in
Wild and weary but working
Act with great abandon
I lay it to bed
Tucked it in cosy
Switched it to silent
Wondered IF ONLY
I could do this every day
To stop purging on thought
To sign a cross in the noughts
I act with great abandon

'Stop calling, I'm doing okay.'

Captions

Cigarettes don't taste the same
For minutes I don't know my name
My legs feel weak until I'm drunk
So this is it
I'm here I'm done

I try to turn it to something new
As though pain is a commodity
Lacking in inspiration
Struggling
This is the truth.

Priorities

I take comfort in the kisses
Not the real ones
No.
The digital missives
The Xs
The exes
An equal amount would be enough
Would I be so fucked up?
If I wanted to be text
As much as I needed to be loved.

Busy

In the darkest solitude
I'm still here, still me
Still available
To anyone who wants a piece
In the quiet, wrapped away
From first thing in the morning
Throughout the whole damn day
Even when I want some space
Or feel guilty taking it up
Even when I'm busy and stressed
Even when I'm making it up
To seem important
An innocent pressurised style of fraudulence
It's all one big fat lie
Really
I've forgotten how it feels to be alone
Or any independent feeling
I miss being lonely
Disconnected from being so connected
Never having a moment
To feel affected, dejected,
I've redefined rejected
From lack of being wanted

But before I know it
Phone calls, texts and WhatsApps
Tweets and likes and hearts to hand
Noise
It doesn't stop
I am held to be a subservient speaking piece
To something I can't turn off.

Switching Off

It burns. Half acid reflux, half Chinese wrist twist in the pit of my stomach. Momentarily, it pops and pings and it leaves my fists to clench tight around the plastic casing until I hurtle it across the room.

Please don't smash.

Please don't be important.

My fear of texts, emails, calls, notifications has now become physical. It's difficult to explain without likening the incoming vibration to a giant mythic monster that wants to devour me. I am reduced to this now, my internal monologue, my internal rhetoric, so obvious, so clichéd, so ready to be condensed into 160 characters. I feel trivialised by my own voice. 'Giant mythic monster that wants to devour me', what part of my brain did I just engage to think that sounded smart or profound? A box left cerebrally Sellotaped shut from the age of six? Give me strength.

Oh.

Off I go on a tangent.

What was making me miserable again?

Shit. It's ringing again. Even if I know it's a friend asking for coffee, my brain re-translates that information and swells it into panic. Hot nasty panic.

Unknown number?

Hell. No.

WhatsApp party invite?

I'm busy.

Text from a colleague?

I don't exist anymore.

At what point can I kid myself that, through being so drastically difficult to get hold of, I just don't exist? At what point does that become true? Whilst it is painful and boring for me, I am relentlessly scared of what others must make of it.

Rudeness.

Ignorance.

Callous, uncalled-for ghosting.

It's sad because it's not personal. I just find it so hard.

So hard.

Sometimes I imagine a life where I just didn't have a phone. Perhaps then I'd stop having to usher pitiful excuses months later about why I never called back. It's so far removed from care, from social interaction, that I can't get my head in or around it. I scroll my contacts when I make it into London to see who I can call for lunch.

No one.

I have avoided 80% of these numbers for months, why on earth would they want to eat the lunch I starved them of in February?

Shit, did I even cancel?

I am someone who constantly strives to avoid loneliness – I like the noise and clatter of loud chatter around a dinner table, I like being near people, I like exchanging stories and I like being a part of jokes and I like my friends. I like them a lot. So why has my phone made me so phobic? I just can't face it.

Occasionally I'll see a set of months where I'm relatively unfazed, engaged in midnight texting and meme shares, but currently I'm not there. It is quick to escalate. One missed call becomes one unread text which then becomes another and another and another and another day of dread and fear that I've not replied.

Now I have to be silent on social media. I can't seem to be engaging in other parts of the digital world.

Then a week goes by and I've not posted a picture of my breakfast or reshared a pointed political article. Then sixty emails pour in.

Open one. Muster a reply, perhaps text one of 19 unread texts, promise drinks next Tuesday.

Facebook messenger pings.

Commit to dinner on Wednesday.

Monday comes and I am scared and exhausted again.
Cancel all plans.
Turn phone back off.
Repeat.
What's this inane bollocksing idiocy?
What's the under layer?
Anyone?
Does anyone know?

Maybe I should just keep it switched off.

Broken Abacus

I move my rings
From right to left
Like playing with an abacus
One finger with a perfect tan
The other pale in new absence
Absence
Abstinence
Passionless
By accident
Had not given it much analysis
But suddenly I'm stuck in a psyche paralysis
When the guy who's plonked down next to me at the bar
Surveys me
'Oh babe, you look fabulous
What are you drinking?'
And it's not that I am thankless
Nor was he particularly tactless
I fancied him, I really did
Absolutely no denying his handsomeness
Had this been 2017, this is where the night would've turned
      quite scandalous
But I move my rings
From right to left
Like playing with an abacus
'Sorry darling, I'm engaged
But I appreciate the compliment.'
His eyes swing off from optimist and dominant
Now bitter, soured, unimpressed
He moves his seat and splutters 'boring'
I don't know why I did it but
I think maybe it's less morbid
To suggest I've already found love instead of

'I just don't have time for a mortgage.'
'I'd love a baby but I don't think I can afford it.'
'What if we do this for three months more
And you still won't call me your girlfriend?'
'Have a drink with you and fall in love and leave unscathed?'
'You're a man not a godsend.'
When did it all become life admin?
So confusing, complex, tricky
What happened to enchantment?
Oxytocin banging like confetti cannons
Having a traditional life trajectory
Imagine
I wonder if I had gone to school
Then university
Found my sweetheart
Then a flat
Got married, had a baby
Worked until I was 65
And died a few years later
If that was all a possibility
If that was attainable and expected of me
I'd leave my rings
Not need to count on them
But as one hand clasps my phone
And my fake engagement rock glistens
I realise I'd been so consumed by frustration
When fate called, I picked up but didn't listen
Romance used to start in bars
But I'd grown so used to the comfort of a screen
'WAIT, COME BACK. I'M SINGLE.'
I flap about and scream
But he's gone
The room fills with his
Absence

My abstinence
Passionless
By accident
I think I've got a broken abacus
Because none of this adds up
And none of this should matter.

Overshare

Personal and political
Controversial and hospitable
Frightened and empowered
Sleeping safer, but for hours
Pushing it out, locking it in
Fumbling for the end of the anecdote
Before it's had time to set in
Renting out space for others to sit
When all I want is a new one
Because this home is still sick.

She Must Be Mad

Introduction

For the men who broke my heart, for the beta-blockers that slowed it, and a chunk of what is left to the sisterhood with a gift tag wrapped around it reading: let's try and figure this all out together.

I owe this all to my madness and those who have suffered it. I never thought I'd be a poet. I never knew one day I'd slap a title on a cover that encased sometimes lonely and sometimes excited thoughts and say, 'Here it is! A book of poems! By me, Charly ... The Poet!' But life shocks you and here we all are. In that never tense, I didn't know a thing – I just knew how to feel. I took to feeling like a sport and I exercised every one of those achy heartstrings that had festered in cliché drivel until they snapped and aortic wells poured and shouted, 'For god's sake woman, can you just write these feelings down so we can have a break?' And so I did. For years in silence and secrecy. I wrote these poems and letters to my past self and in every sort of melodramatic, romantic, ridiculous way, these are what saved me. Saved me from an intensity I was afraid to share until I morphed them into something to share with you now. Some of these were written at sixteen, others at twenty-two; they were all written growing and lost and sad sunk, but they were also all written with eventual hope. A hope that I clung to in the most intense way that only a girl desperate to take a peek at womanhood, battling a wealthy portfolio of mental health issues nervously, could. Finding strength in the contention of such frustrated confusion, in odd and debilitating sadness, in jubilant first kisses and clangs of clarity – in the words of our lord saviour Britney Spears, 'I'm not a girl – not yet a woman'. And there is something truly quite almighty in that in-between ... either that or, I must truly just be mad.

She Must

Be
in Love

Love Part 1

Nobody ever tells you that there'll be comedians and poets, actors and academics, college students and forty-year-old men to fall in love with.

That you will fall in love with them all.

Their charm and their poise, their anecdotes and foreign phrases, even the stray scratchy hairs on their cheeks and chins that will tickle like an acrylic yarn against your youth.

They first come soft. Soft and slow and ethereal, these perfumed clouds of promise that smell new but hang old, and then before a single tendril has had time to make itself at home on your collar, they exit loud and angry and too early.

They will always exit too early.

Little-to-no explanation, a hole so deep you lose your feet to the black and bleak of self-assumed guilt, he flings the door on its hinges for another man to oil and mend.

You'll re-imagine hope until he leaves too, tarnishing his very own handiwork.

Nobody ever tells you of these good-looking silhouettes because they have stood in their cast before. They relished in the same way you will but they cowered in the flood.

They sunk with weakened limbs until they no longer knew of that initial burst and lay themselves down to surrender. You, however, will not allow yourself to be a casualty to love. You will grow stronger in it, if you try.

It's six minutes past midnight, Facebook has updated Messenger, video now available, you have no one to call.

Soon, it's twenty-one minutes past twelve and an unfamiliar noise rings through the hard plastic of your first laptop, it starts to screech.

You look up and to the side, a rerun of the news now only important to your periphery.

A boy. It's a boy.

A boy you've never met but whose life you know the lengths of. Holidays, parties, girlfriends, new friends, birthdays, likes, lunches – all arranged into bite-sized books you've read and torn pages from time and time again. The boy. The boy from the holidays and the parties, with the girlfriends and the new friends, he's calling you.

You answer.

Spanking new anticipation twirling twines that tie knots in your chest, frayed ends tickling your stomach to stir hot queasy butterfly soup.

'Hello.' He says, monotone. Northern.

Eyes thinning to an embarrassed sleepy squint.

'Hey?' You say, a question. Southern.

Smile curving to bunch the bags from under your eyes to pillows.

'Just wondered what your voice sounded like.' He says, he smiles back.

'Same. Now we know.'

Lights dim in both screens, you dissolve into the silence of each other's nights, minds reaching out to touch the other, tousle hair, feel skin. Talk. Talk. Laugh. Smile.

Embarrassment has gone.

It's five thirty-six in the morning four years later. Lights still dim, faces still rounded in the glow of the laptop. Girlfriends once stalked are now ex-girlfriends discussed. Holidays, planned as fleeting dreams of train journeys across the country to finally meet. Likes, shared. Sometimes agreed.

'Do we know, or at least think, that if you lived down the road from me we'd be in love?' He wrote.

'Yes.' You reply.

A life starts to lead along a parallel secret line, a life that's yours and a line of fibre optics. Two years pass. You meet in a newsagent at a train station. He's smaller than you thought. You're fatter than he'd seen. Geography offers different greetings. Kiss, hug, release. You share pancakes but struggle to look at each other. You walk across Battersea Bridge, he lights a spliff, you sit facing away from each other and imagine you're still just on the phone. Better.

Three years later and it has never happened again. You never found out if he became the poster boy for postmen in Salford. You never got to tell him of the new bosses and the trips to America. You never got to tell him all the things he was right about. You never got to tell him how your heart held out, how it still occasionally chooses to hold out. How in a life lived on a parallel secret line you never unplugged the receiver. But now you do. Now you get to tell him somewhere he might find it and can only hope he does, before he finds someone else.

I called him out of
the blue to tell him I'd
written this. He downloaded
the free audio version and
played it to women to...
'impress them'.
We fell out - I found
my worth. But truly i'd not change
a thing.

To You

This feels silly to write
For in doing so
The sentiment fractures
And goes back full circle
But I've kissed plenty of boys
Most of them charming
I've kissed plenty of boys
And I've been on plenty of arms and
I've loved plenty of boys
And they've made me feel soft
And I've seen plenty of boys
And plenty I've lost
I've had plenty of evenings
In dimly lit bars
And I've had plenty of fumbles
In the backs of their cars
I've written plenty of letters
And received plenty of emails
I've kissed plenty of boys
And one or two females
I've traced plenty of hips
With eager touch
And I've kissed plenty of lips
That made me feel too much
And in the plenty I've gathered
I've garnered plenty of words
But once put all together
They don't sound like firsts
They all sort of sound similar
As though each man wasn't new
Which is why it's important to say
Not everything I write is about you.

She Moves In Her Own Way

It was sticky in your apartment
I stuck my eyes to every corner
Where you'd stuck up old postcards
An entire museum of your life and more a
Window
Framed the shrilling stuck-up summer silhouettes in the pub
    down below
You stuck a scratched record on
That played the once smooth staccato
You poured me a glass of wine
That slipped sticky to my sides
That slipped your fingers across my thighs
I felt stuck
This time I promised myself I wasn't giving up
You said stick around
And I cleared off the dark sediment red wine muck
From my lips
And kissed you in a way
That begged to reverse ownership
But instead it sellotaped my wrists
Together tight around your hips
Whilst my internal monologue screamed:
You're hopeless at this
You don't want to do this
You always do this
You don't have to be this
Person
You don't have to quench your thirst on
Him
Tell your body its anxiety isn't a passion to burst on
Him
Don't try and fill the void with empty consumption
This moment in time that you'll lie and say was sweet seduction

Was another episode of you orchestrating a personality reduction
Into a girl you have no business being
No pleasing being
Stop teasing feeling
From an inner drought
That only dried to be that way
Because you gave all your kindness out
Instead of spending it on yourself.

I stop as your eyes unstuck from mine
You swig from the bottle of wine
And I muster up the courage to say
I don't want to be just tonight
I've said it before and let it be denied
And you laugh with a cocksure sigh
And hit me with another line like
Why can't you just be a girl for a good time?
And it's the just that juts
And ricochets
And it slaps stuck
To my ongoing conflict with myself
　　　I reach for a souvenir placed on your shelf
Throw it between my palms
Imagine what false comfort I'd find within your arms
And put it back
I give learning from lessons a crack
I stop myself from telling you that you're such a twat
When you text me the next morning
To say my excuse as a woman is appalling
For leaving in a rush
It was sticky in your apartment
And it was there that I realised
I was bored of being stuck
As a girl whose muchness amounted to just
The night.

[handwritten note:] As glam as celeb dating apps sound – Raya was only good for two things. 1. Terrible men you fancied in your teens 2. Poetry

Mourning Routine

He is unsmoked cigarettes
And lukewarm tea
A morning routine
(He's) not consumed by me
A craving that will fade
Left unfinished in the sink
Until my wine-stained lips
Call the next round of drinks

I'll wake up in the morning
Next to someone new
But I still fell asleep
Hoping that someone would be you.

Mesh of
Kisses

Find the contented without the contention of giving away half
of yourself
And see that letting go isn't giving in
But a spiritual commodity of wealth
My best teachers were disguised as lovers
Unmasked when I untangled their mesh of kisses
And smothered myself instead with the notion that they were
knowledgeable near misses
And Mr Brave
The future without the listless lustful nights
Replaced with a silhouette of love
That was bred from moulding a mistreated wrong into its
rightful right.

Anatomical Astrologist

Your body became so familiar
I touched your skin the same way I'd fumble down the side of
    the TV in the dark and know the difference between the
    <off switch> and the <volume button>
Each line and freckle a constellation on your torso
        I could read backwards like an anatomical astrologist.
            We intertwine and I sigh softly
           a shared unspoken bedtime language that
                screamed
              to the gods for just
                  five
                more
              minutes
Time stopped to matter and the matter of us across your old
    mattress pulled apart until your stars dimmed down to
    flickering filaments and I chose to switch them off.

Otters

It is what it is until it isn't
Quite it anymore
Makes perfect logical sense, sure
But in eleven short words I don't think you swirl the score
Of what I'm on about
I could mutter an uttering of offers
Words that cling to syllables as tightly as otters
In love
Did you know they never let go once they've found a mate?
Did you know that my slithering of truth wasn't yours
        to emanate
Dissipate, dissolve upon your lips
As my truth became a movement and your hands
        became my hips
In a haze of a few Sundays
Of what I thought was it
But didn't know that it could be something just one of us
        could quit
And that's quite exactly it
It was what it wasn't
Instead of a smattering of emails that will one day be forgotten
Instead of a flattering string of inhales that sung kindly until
        coughed out rotten.
Again these are all just words
Silly sold sentiments aren't that tough
I could rhyme anything together and it'd still be enough
For you to know what I'm wittering on about is love
It is what it is until it isn't
Quite it anymore
It's tracing your finger on a back
That will soon traipse out the door
It's wine on a Saturday and lies that you learn as foreplay

It's lust in its golden hour
It's kissing goosebumped in the shower
It's handing over innocence to a dastardly power
Of frightening fragile fragments that someone can stack in
      their own tower
No choice in whether it cements a building for their ego or a
      fence around a field of flourishing flowers
All grown for you
It is what it is until it isn't quite it anymore
Until you become loathsome for the quibbling quirks
      of comfort
And love writes as a rule to deplore
Makes perfect logical sense, sure
Until the it that isn't and the was that wasn't
Is just a silhouette of your insecurity
And truly nothing more.

Weight of You

As my body writhes around a different bed
It feels taller even though it's not
Semi-clothed and cold it feels different
But not lonely
It feels older and as though it knows further and fresh
It learns less of you and no wider of me
But it understands something new
That isn't uncomfortable
It just wants to find you again and for you to know
      me once more
And for that once more to see what I wished you'd seen before

Before it would cry out a screech of heart strung bedlam
Lying with a bread-bloated belly that looked pregnant
Pregnant with the thought of you
Coming back to bed soon
But you didn't

Different cities and marbled skies
Slow the pace between us
And Indian spices heat the burn our tongues loved together
But now saffron and chai
Taste an unsavoury uncleanness

There is no loneliness to chew
Just a space in the creases of linen
That should belong to the weight of you.

Lipstick

Let me kiss you close mouthed
Let me rouge your bitter cheeks
With this darker red
Let me wrap the gentle curve of my body
Into someone else's bed
I'll let you wipe the cherry plum stain off
With the memory of when you said
'Cheer up sweetheart, the thing with
People like you, is they'll only love you
When you're dead.'

Lovebites

I hadn't noticed it at first
It was done with such kindness
It hadn't thought to hurt
But as I stumble off the train
With my knickers hitching my skirt
It would've been nice to know of the night
That instead of just leaving my phone charger behind
I'd be taking away a lovebite
A 'hickey'
A purple blue yellow not nearly skin-coloured enough to cover
With make-up
Tricky
Situation
Learning to flatten my tones from their guilty
       high fluctuations
When I say
It's eczema?!
At school a girl had one on her head
And said
She'd headbutted a cupboard
And cut in a fringe before the teachers had discovered it
Is so silly that they must be hidden
That something which once brought pleasure
Is suddenly forbidden
Like, grossly forbidden
Like, I walked into a party and everyone was shocked
That I was either bursting with pride
Or should be embarrassed that I'd forgot
To slap on some concealer
Or that I was akin to a slapper who'd hooked up with a
       drug dealer
Which for the record would be fine

It's my neck to be decorated by whomever I desire
Minutes of passion holstered to a circle
That gets flashed every now and again
Like being autographed with a biological purple pen
It's a bruise from a kiss
Not a place keeper for a fist
Just a splodge of romance stamped profoundly pissed
It's as fleeting as the youth we're scared to miss
As it's administered
I struggle to cast it off as something sinister

And for whatever attention they seem to seek
I'm happy to laugh in their existence
And thank god that they only last a week.

With His Assistants

some things are worth forgetting an NDA for...

She squirms nearly naked beside me
Lollipop stick legs
Like a Lowry
Waiting to be coloured
I fill her in best I can
With a haze-hugged recital
Madness over just one man
It splutters slurred and sloppy
I feel her skin soft and on me
She breathes a sigh drenched in
Yawns for coffee
We put on one of his shirts together
Find the slunked-off socks
And bury down secrets we now have to keep forever
His face is unimaginable
He'd have guessed it sooner
Had his lust been made more tangible
But he was busy
When we were busy for him.

Doubletree by Hilton

Mesmeric in the most disarming demanding way
I flash honesty brazen and wasted
As you kiss the words from out my mouth as though they're
    still untasted
Satiated
We lay
As you press your head upon me and lie about my beauty as
    though it's your unspoken duty
I feel safe because you've said it
Feel a rush of adrenaline and then push it from my head
You said it
I watched you close your eyes and forget it for a second
And then deny it
You falsify your worth with memories unjust
You try nothing more than to make me feel I was
    once untouched
And now all I want
Is for the history before us
To erase in diluted drops
That you slipped along my index fingers
When in this heat my rings got stuck.

Porn

She moans
As he throws
Her body
From arched feline back
To face in the pillow on her tummy
He pulls her by the ponytail
Her eyes widen with excitement
Loneliness
As well
Banshee screams and hollow slaps
Perfect nudity and waxed arse cracks
Half taken by the throng of flung-off thongs
I'm bemused and sad and thinking
Why do they never show the naps?
The intimate legs twined like spaghetti
Cooked and thrown back in the pack
Stuck with starchy love
That's the real magic, that
That's what turns me on
When after all the sheets have seen
Where you lay and nose touches nose
And you still know where to kiss
With the lights still off
Because you're lit up in a childlike beam
And through panting pause your mind wanders lost
Feeling your skin cling innate to one another
Like a baby to a breast
                            That first breath
When you exhale and simmer,
Two maudlin corpses
Too hot and they still shiver
Craving more whilst digesting a slither

Of moments ago

She moans
As he throws
Her body
Wanting it with a posture comfy
He runs his fingers through her hair
And tells her that she's lovely
Beautiful in fact
He grabs her by the waist
As she holds his face
And steadies gaze
Whispers lightly in his ear
I'd rather make love to you
Than just simply let you fuck me

There is plenty of room for explicits in complicity

Now *that* I'd understand
A prude I'd never claim to be
Though nor a connoisseur of wild intimacy
I've always taken it how it's given to me
... directed it occasionally
But there's something that seems strange to me
That we get off on a close-up of a staged aggressive filthy
When we all know in reality
The best is sweet and purely
Ends the same
The two of you, vulnerable and glowing
With the taste of each other's name.

Evolution

Days later
Paint-like
Each layer peels
And falls from my lips
That you bit
And thus become features
That are no longer owned by your kiss.

Snapple Lid Facts

An octopus has three hearts
How does he find time to use them?
Dexterous in his tentacle touch
It must be hard to know what's a tickle from abuse to them
What space there is for entertaining a mermaid or a sea urchin
He doesn't have to unpick beauty from sense or
      smarts from lust
He can just drink them all up
In a salty ablution
And sit drunk
Sounds nice but
I bet it's secret emotional hassle
I bet he'd prefer to slurp a sluice of Snapple
What decisions are necessary to make when there's a home for
      each mistake
All kept warm and left unsearching
How does he find time to use them when he needs it all just
      to keep them working?
Keep each beat in syncopation
Without disrupting the sea's heady and unforgiving intention
Selling him gravelly bits of information
As he presses his ear to a shell
How does he decide what's worth keeping or best shelved?
How does he pick what's right and fulfilling

When he's got three beating organs never fit to burst or to be
      pained and unspilling
How does he feel anything
When he's got capacity for so much?
Squirming neatly on the sea bed
He stretches out to disturb the dust
Half swim half sleep he imagines what it would be like to be us

How simple it could be
To reserve all of his energy
Into just one place to love.

Kaleidoscope

As you bashed my eyes from blue
These distorted shapes were carved by you
Until swiftly all I saw judged hope
As you threw me in your kaleidoscope
Pushed down a misted barrel lens
Creasing wraps and crushing tenths
Squinting smiles as you kissed wrists
and squaring miles on homebound trips
I wandered calm for months before
Became the girl you swore unsworn
And now headfirst it smacks me clean
You conjured colours I can't see
A fool I often am
But tonight a fool I'll gladly be.

Rosie Cheeks

It smells as delicious
As my mind told me so
And as its thorns graze my thigh
I apologise before its beauty
And cry not for pain
But for getting too close
To something much more delicate than I
And not expecting to leave bloodied.

App Cheats

Their names together wash over me
Syncopated
Hypnotic
Tepid water rushes through my sinuses
Until it heats to a gentle boil
Slow bubble, rising
To sit along my lash line
As a stagnant source
Awaiting provocation
Syncopated
Hypnotic
Vindicated and
Neurotic
I almost wanted them to
Sound like a flood
I scrounge for photos of
Them in love
I rip through feeds
And rehash texts
And play out what
He didn't say next
As though he did
I am crazed by the drama
That has been denied
And scroll through three years of holiday photos
That he profiled as a lie.

First West Service

He pressed his palms against my breasts
On a crowded bus
Cradling the darkness in my head
Until it felt like it was just us
And when we got back to his
In solitude we could melt
I went to tell him who I was
But learnt he wasn't there for how I felt.

You sit with your tongue pained out of your mouth like an artist, bottle of stolen rum from your parents' cabinet in one hand and an emptied bottle of water between your thighs.

Don't. Spill. Anything.

You learned only last night that Malibu has a particularly unforgiving stench when left to soak in carpet. Neatly, you tuck it into your school bag, pocket four pound coins from your father's parking meter compartment in his Volvo estate and head to school on a cold Friday morning. The night is young. The night is so young you're checking for spillage in double maths and texting a boy from the school down the road 'wuu2 tonight?' with one eye on algebra and the other on your LG Shine phone. You know what he's up to.

It feels like the longest day of your life, in hindsight nothing really does ever feel as long as today. You are a worthy warrior that fights each pounding heart thump of anxious anticipation in her stride, you valiantly navigate the hours with nothing but a muted floral bodycon skirt and silk low-cut top awaiting to be loaded as ammunition.

The day dribbles off into the later afternoon and you salivate to evening, thirsty dry mouth puckering in your mother's lipgloss.

The prolonged MSN chat has been aching, tension-building, near nausea. Tonight you'll have your first kiss. You know it, you can see it, you have dreamt enough *Angus, Thongs and Perfect Snogging* scenes, it will be tonight. It must be. You feel so terrifyingly far behind that if it's not, womanhood will never greet you. You are not a girl nor a woman, you are an unwanted potato in a packet, left to half-freeze too close to the back of the fridge. It must be tonight. The process prior is almost ceremonial, the half a beer that leaves you giddy is a toast to the gods of fate, the borrowed pair of tanned tights is your celebration wear, the panic attack in the locked bathroom of the party before you've met is a nod and a vow to the severity of the process. It's all quite dumb, all quite ridiculous, all quite right. The party is quickening in pace, the toilet door you have bolted is being kicked at to make way for an early casualty of apple sours, you steady your defences and anchor a root in a confidence you have grown in that moment. Animalistic in your approach, you sidle past each faux drunken swaying body, pushing through a living room, a kitchen, and then to a garden with purpose. There he is. Too tall in his body he has not yet grown into, he leans on a trellis in the rain. You say your name at him like a greeting. He nods, accepting, watching your Bebo user flash before his squinted eyeline. You talk. It is all so unbearably awkward that you look for other familiar faces you can slope off with. You slope off with him. Backs against a forgotten Wendy house, you kiss. It's unlike anything. No metaphor, no simile, no book you read too young. It's tongues and hot flushed panic, it's anxiety boiled to a surface of pure sugar resin that you bite from each other's lips.

It's a morishness sans lust, it feels innate. It feels as though there is an end point you must discover but you only have the tools to enquire and not conquer. It is feeling without thought for the first time. It's delicious – brief flashes of mortified and embarrassed – but delicious. No kiss will ever be the same. Some more prolific, some more dramatic, some more regretful, some more meaningful. But none the same. None more swift and intoxicating. None that was so unashamedly stenched with a mud-stained half hangover that when you head to text him the next morning, the ambush of 'WAHEEEEEEEY!!! I SAW YOU LAST NIGHT!!' splashed across your Facebook wall lights you with unabashed pride that nothing else will ever give you. You later realise, much much later, that the grin that lasted for weeks was the end of all those months of feeling like 'the fat friend', 'the nerd in disguise', 'the uncool one', 'the forgettable one'. They were all sad endured lies because within those was 'the girl that would never be kissed'. And she was. And she would be again.

The First Time

Numbed nerves and conceited confidence
We fall into a depth of expectation
Familiarity grins back at us
And it laughs
And we laugh
Complexities lace around your features
Truth curling through my tongue
Slicing through a mist of excitement
Spilling to curdle into bittersweet reality

Mistaken as a mistake

As your slow body collapses
Next to me I watch your mind spin
Tentative teeth caging your thoughts
Until we digress into secrets
Misjudged, misinterpreted, mishaps

We are wondering
You are lost and I have lost.

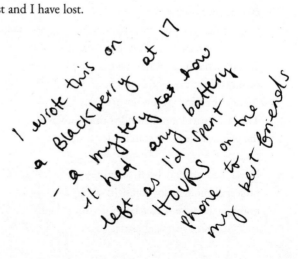

I wrote this on a Blackberry at 17 - a mystery as how it had any battery left as I'd spent HOURS on the phone to my best friends

Love Part 2

Love is going to smack you in such a way you don't recognise it, from the hands of a man whose fingers you wouldn't trust on a trigger. Love isn't what you thought. It's not what you were ever expecting. In your twenties, naked body sprawled across someone's bathroom, throwing up all within you, listening to the clink of plates as he toasts you crumpets having just cleaned up your mess, you muster, 'I love you.' Weird. Uncomfortable. What?! It's all too much to fathom. Surely you can't be that basic? It changes.

One night, when you are in his bed, his hot sticky breath scalds your skin with a thick jamminess, it prickles quick temperate flashes along your neckline and you begin to cry. You reimagine all the times he stopped to take your photograph. 'What are you doing? I look so gross, stop it. What sort of memory is this?!' You'd bat, pulling strands of hair from behind your ears over your face to hide. 'It's only for me!' Only for him? You could never quite grasp why anyone would want a collection of pictures of you with burnt rosacea red cheeks, often hungover, in his pyjama tops, in budget cafés, until right now. It stings you as he leans to kiss you and you can't pucker because all you can do is cry. It's not really even a cry, it's a sob. A snot on your chin, belly aching screech of water works. He is confused. His gentle comforting strokes force your body rigid. 'I'm fine, I'm fine, just change the song. It always makes me sad.' This is partly true. The other part loops behind your eyelids as you press them into the pillow as he panic searches for something new. It won't stop.

Never had an end been so grotesquely visceral. Never had a projected moment of foresight clung to your brain as though nothing else would ever be more true. When would anyone sit and look through such bizarre, such random, such inane photos?

When you were no longer there.

You see his limbs half in and half out, snaked around his duvet weeks from now. His finger pinching to zoom, swiping furiously through months. Looking at all these moments that at the time you thought were nothing of note but now are all that remain.

The tears slowly start to lessen, he gives you a lost stare and you offer a half smile. Dimples that suggest you know you're being silly. Silly for crying over 'a song'.

But in reality, there was not an ounce of silliness or stupidity to your reaction. You'd planned tomorrow's walk, you'd planned the lunch you'd attempt to eat, you'd planned the words you'd say to him, to explain this wasn't working any more, you had planned the whole damn thing and suddenly in a wisp of an unexpected thought, all those plans unravelled and you won't stomach it for weeks.

Even now, looking back, thinking on the countless photos taken after that night, you wished you'd taken some too. You wished you'd smiled in a few. You wished you'd had half the heart you had that night to have made an effort or, at least, to have been honest sooner.

Love is also continued frustration. It's anger. It's hurting. It's denying it for months and only seeing its presence, for the first time, in a memory. It is not always just the butterfly chase that you expected. Sometimes it's also resentment. It's embarrassment. It's putting all of your dreams on hold, totally swept in not realising. It's endurance. It's anguish. It's not what you wanted, not what you went looking for in your absent search for the next thing. It's intoxicating, it's routine, it's hard goddamn work. But they don't tell you that. Or maybe they do. Maybe you weren't listening. Maybe you were hanging off the end of a feeling late night WhatsApps gave you. Hanging off the end of movies, of prematurely-written poetry you'd penned in hope of one day arriving there with a person. It's horrid. It's gross. It's real and it stinks in a romantic putrid parma violet sweetness. So today you hate yourself for thinking you knew what love was but when it arrived you couldn't send it back quick enough. Laying in your pants on the sofa with last night's curry reheated screaming to no one but the ceiling.

'I DIDN'T ASK FOR THIS. THIS ISN'T IT.
HOW DO I RESIGN?'

But no matter how many times you swipe with wool-gathered ease through Tinder praying to erase it, no matter how many times you tweet your soul is a dark expanse and your heart is a gothic black cave in as many self-depreciating retweet-worthy characters, it isn't. Your heart is filled with chest banging love and there is absolutely nothing you can do about it and that is it. Love is 'that is it' even when you feel like it isn't.

She Must

Be Mad

Mind Part 1

You remember, quite explicitly, the moments all of the weight first felt tangible. Your best girlfriend from school blimps in on MSN, 'I love you but I don't think I can help you anymore.' Each word sinks and anchors ground to the pit of your stomach and steadies your defences. She is right. A week later your best male friend bikes in the snow to your house at two-thirty in the morning and you let him cradle you as your apologies splutter out with a stench of lavender bleach. Weeks before, scissor scores sloped around the shapes of the tips of your fingers so you could no longer hold a pen on exam day. You lay, heavy in limbs and mind, cursing that no one else had ever felt this way. No one could understand. There wasn't a name for you, so you create a face instead. Bright and brash, loud and lovely – you walk into every room with conversation, jokes, anecdotes, bold red lipstick, and funny styled hair. You swig from bottles of wine and ring in every party as the go-to girl for a good time. It is much easier this way. Nobody has to know. MSN has long folded, your teeth cleansed from bathroom cleaner, the hard skin on your hands now, just simply, interesting. It's a charade that becomes so well-scripted, lovingly rehearsed, articulated in mirrors of bars before re-entering, that often it is hard to decipher which part of you is acting. You forget so quickly in those performances, of the excruciating pain, the sobbing, the fast heart racing to leap from out your chest via your mouth and spluttered in bile before you can leave the house. You deny yourself that those moments were true and that they ever happened. You attend doctors' appointments, pop pills, dutifully research a Wikipedia file of celebrities with 'bipolar II', scream at your friends, scream at the chemist, scream at the man in the bloody corner shop, scream at yourself that even though the weight still feels tangible, it can't be real. You are solemnly bored of pity, of being bedridden ... of performing. Advisors come and go, all wearing different masks, some lovers, some friends, some professionals, your costume remains the same until one day you sit in front of a girl with deep purple hair and pink lipstick. She orders you a bowl of mash potato and a side of broccoli, an espresso and a Bloody Mary. She holds your hand and tells you the one thing that everybody else had given you with guilt but this time gives it to you as a gift. It feels warm, it's cosy cuddled relief. It's the truth and this time it isn't lonely.

'You're not well. You're ill. You're suffering. It's all real, all of this. I'm here to help you see it through.'

Thank GOD|||| for Scarlett . . .

'She Must Be Mad'

They called me many things
In many places
All well-intentioned
Muffled nouns spluttered from kind faces
Adjectives
Then descriptors
Ushering packets of pills and tales of other strong victors
Sympathetic sighs and brushed smiles
With trying advice to dissolve difficult enmeshed vices
They all said things would get better
To treat this thing as a workable quirk and not an evil
      personal personality vendetta
That I had in for myself
Try loving yourself
And when you do tell others how
The journey you've been on is another girl's now
Another kid just like you pressing their brain
      shouting owwww
The honesty will hurt a bit, it might make you sad
But ignite a spark that burns brighter
Than all of the times you heard
'She must be mad',
Ignite a spark that burns brighter
Than all of the hurt
To smile
'Yeah, I guess I am, but it isn't all bad.'
Ignite a spark that burns brightest
From all of the dirt
The dribbling tear-sodden thirst
To drink to the girl you knew
She must be mad but my god she's brave too.

@saintrecords

When sanity seems so far
And guarded by gates made of worries
I thank a god
I wish were true
For Solange's Instagram stories.

Doctor, Doctor, Don't Help Me

(written aged 15)

I think I crave rejection
And self-sabotage days
I like the way they taste
In their smokey beer cross haze
I like to feel this empty
To make some time for pain
Nothing drives me more crazy
Than the breaks of feeling sane.

Selective
Feeling

Sometimes I forget I'm totally insane
But then I'll start to hear voices
And remember again
I don't want to be crazy
But sometimes there's comfort
In that's my word for lazy
Or sad
Or defeated
Or bouncing off walls
And I think if I wasn't
I'd find myself bored.

I Wish I'd Not Spent So Long Crying In Bed

I fear too much
To quantify the rest
To feel the beat
With flat palms on my chest
I fear too much
To think back to
When I wanted less
I fear too much
To see the mess
Of how much time I wasted
When I had plenty left.

Rapid Cycling

You put stars in my shoes
And clouds in my head
I'd chase the moon
If I could get out of bed

If I could slap my feet flat
On the floor
And walk towards
What you allotted yesterday
You hand me my fleeting allowance
Of disgruntled energy
So I can feel the thick winter air
Like a cold second skin
That blows through the splinters in the trees
And the cracks you've chiseled within

The fluctuating curves of bowing branches
Are the sunken eyes nestled under furrowed arches

You gift a still minute
And then gallop off with it
Always a step ahead
And just a scant visit.

Funny

I feel *funny*.
Not like when – the light bounces from the sky
And you feel heat stroke from the sunny
Days of closing in on jokes
That girl is intelligently witty she's so *funny*
I feel done in
Funny 'ha ha's speak no fun
In the language I have learnt
Funny feelings aren't the taste of a jovial summer's eve descending burn
A *funny* feeling is a feeling of a leaf I'm scared to turn
A *funny* feeling is me seething at a friend
Who didn't mean to hurt
Me, I'm a bit *funny* that way
Funny isn't laughing at a joke I heard you say
Funny is me cramping in the lungs and wincing
I'm okay
Funny is the last thought before I sleep
Funny is the impression of me that you'll keep
Funny is the unexplained, self-contained
Anxiety of breathing
Grabbing my coat before closing
Because I feel *funny* as I'm leaving
That's why I'm leaving
I feel strange
A finger couldn't pinpoint it and words cannot explain
The curse of feeling *funny*
And knowing you've got yourself to blame
And still being unaware.
I took my pills this morning, I promise you I swear
The capsules grin at you in blister packs
And eyeless they still stare
They laugh at you

Like you've said something *funny*
There's no lies that you can throw at them
There's no amount of money

No words you can scream
Out
Bluntly.
I've tried
Feeling so funny that *funny* isn't hysterical
So why am I crying hysterical tears?
Funny was something I'd always liked
So why does this *funny* feeling punch me with spite?
A funny feeling used to be the swig of a third pint
So why does feeling *funny* swing the last throw in my own fight?
If I stopped feeling *funny* maybe I'd get some sleep at night
I wish someone had shown me left when *funny* started to feel right

And I suppose the *funny* thing is that in life
First we laugh
And then we cope
First we mould aching into satire
And then claw our way into a hope
That the lumps in our throats, the inhalers tucked in
    pockets of coats
The fraying yarns on the tether of our metaphorical ropes
Don't really exist
But they do, I know they do.
And I think they deserve a more raucous applause
Than the monotonous bang of therapists' doors
Or the bedlam screams on bedroom floors
Or the wincing pinches of scissor scores
Funny no longer feels right
Because there is no comedy show in sight
This is real life
And the word is depression

The medical phrases should be shouted in succession
Because for all the days they've made my face nameless
It would help in abundance for them to be shamed less
For me to call them out for who they are
And I know it's wonderful that we've come this far
Forgive me
But
It's unhealthy for us to stick with
Dancing around a denial that nicks its
Legitimacy from camouflaging its pain
Even though I'm the one who picked it
Saying 'I feel Funny' just isn't the same
But I didn't pick this
I was my own brain before this
And that, as a human, I deserve to reclaim
In whatever funny sort of way I can.

I Prescribe You This

The best sort of revenge is to be kind to yourself
To burden yourself with living another day
With nourishing yourself when it feels like you're not worthy
Sabotage the saboteur
Poison the punisher
With positivity
I try and anger unhappy me
With good thoughts
With slow breathing
I cut my teeth on seething
Searing hot flash panics
It's become so familiar
I feel uncomfortable when things aren't bad
It's
Complex
I want the darkness to know it's wanted
But I want my soul to feel less haunted
So I open up
And double bluff
Until synapses sizzle
And confuse self-harm
With self-love.

> **I know that truth is always beautiful**
> **But this is something else**
> **These are the chronicles**
> **Written out from hell**

These are the minutes we keep secret
The times we wished we were someone else
I know that truth is always beautiful
But this is something else
These are the smudged wings of angels
That we'd erase with second chances
These are the fleeting second glances
That led to the stale and baneful
Excuses for not feeling the same
I know that truth is always beautiful
But this is something else
This is a slice of honest living
I wish I could have dressed up for myself.

All I Wanted Was Some Toast

I got a fork stuck in the dishwasher
And now I can't stop crying
Whoever said depression was glamorous
Had clearly never considered dying
Over a peanut butter covered utensil
And that's not the worst of all
The wet clothes hanger fell over
So I punched my fist into a wall
I'd rather smell than have a shower
The thought of socialising is scary
I can't even binge on chocolate
Because 'happy me' cut out dairy
This is boring, I feel knackered,
All I wanted was some toast
But if I can't even handle that
I'm obviously going to die alone.

A Voice I Know

My thoughts run through unpredictable themes
Sometimes it's two conscious streams at once
Sounds fun, huh?
Sounds a bit like drugs, no?
Sounds like in a predominantly losing game of tapping in on
    our own brains
I've accidentally genetically placed my bets and won
Sometimes I don't shun
It
Sometimes there's some fun in it
Sometimes it's nice to look in from the outside
And still stay warm
But other times it's like being one in a team of
    screaming aggressors
And trying to bat away the swarm
That I've assembled
Sometimes it's like punching confidently bare-knuckled
And still being the one that falls down and trembles
Sometimes I don't know who I am
Most of the time I don't know where I stand
And it's in that exact spotlight
It all comes rushing in:
'You don't deserve him!'
'... Wait no, you're cooler!'
'What is this fatty casing around your limbs?'
'... Stop prodding it, you're much smaller
Than you believe!'
'You've got no point in this world!'
'... Shut up, that's your confidence thief!'
'You should stay in bed!'
'... You should take on the world!'
'You look silly in this dress!'

'... When did I become this beautiful girl?'
'You don't know your facts!'
'... Oh my god, you're on fire!'
'He was looking at her not you.'
'... What's not there to be desired?'
It's all a constant conflict
That speeds in every thought
When I don't feel so great
It draws a pencil line above my head
Much shorter than before
It's a voice that refuses to see growth
And then backtracks for a minute
And shouts that I'm taller than most
Sometimes I need it to hear my own stupidity
And sometimes it knocks a sizeable crack in my
        mental fragility
Sometimes it feels like an illness
And other times it feels like a super ability
When I'm alone it's easy to forget I am
Because someone else is nattering away
And if I had control of at least one of these voices
I've got no idea what I'd say
But maybe, it would be
Right or wrong
Fat or thin
An inbetween of all these things
They'll quieten down when you realise
You're as strong to be so tough
To see that all of you's
Enough.

Wonder of Worry

We become the wonder of worry
Greasy in apologies
Slithering around each other's truths
In a perfect eight-shaped double-headed noose
Beer-foamed lips catch glints
And glisten sticky awaiting calm
That wills to be administered mouth to mouth
As hands cover eyes and fingers rest in their brows

We become the wonder of worry
Wandering straight-edged
Slack-lined, tongues untied, holding
On to strawberry-coloured embarrassed
Pink in the cheeks that we rouged from the tint of our
        hearts, hapless
In spirit and gesture
Cursing our history for being a chemical-stained mess
But as you hold me in the crook of your arm and kiss my
        bruised head
Our madness weighs a little less

The wonder of worry is
Teeth teetering trips of silence
Locked lockets swinging open unasked
Wittering over an expectation of now and love passed
Past a parameter to shut down
Slow down, bend down and under through branches
        we've extended
Piling them high and climbing to a peak of united
        front splendid
We become the wonder of worry
A little lost in the unexpected

But as we wonder together the worry becomes fragmented
Halved and shared and further afloat
There is a crescent smile on our lips
And there's nothing left to clear in our throats.

Amber Meal

Wipe a slick of whiskey from your lips
The burning bitter now a tender kiss
It is a supper of divine, an amber meal
A glass to clink that dins out how to feel
And when we fall back together again
Which I'm certain shall be friends
against the odds
Please know
This crash

And cool of rocks is now my home

climb
Because you left me here to   alone.
I thought it wicked
To offer out a space within you without offering its limit
To dilute down all the hours by leaving in a minute
I thought you wicked
But in a mess of this elixir
I still want you to see my splendour and lie within it.

Unidentified Businessman

Did you see his eyes?
The way he looked at me
I've seen that look before
In doctor's receptions and caught them in glass door reflections
That inward moment you look outward to seek a connection
With yourself through someone else

Did you really see them?
Blink and you'll miss it
A piece of ocean blue and an iris sunk in spirit
Querying a view of judgment so explicit
That you want to hold their two pearly glass pebbles
And extract all of their battled past trembles
And kiss it
Smooch the notion of their preconceptions
Cradle an ounce of the perfect they see as imperfections
And make them look the other way
Shoot back a glance
That knocks their sallow tin man stance
To ricochet
To hand on your heart hand over your heart just for a minute
        in his day
A head nod that doubles as a 'I hope you'll be okay'.

Did you see his eyes?
The way he looked at me
I've seen that look before
And selfishly I've greeted them by staring at the floor
Cracking a stranger's reality into one that's ignored
Walking on embarrassed and showing no remorse
All he wanted for a second was a moment out of the self-
        deprecated and absorbed

Moments we all live in
I saw his eyes and the way he looked at me
This time with no pause for thought or time to breathe
I looked down deep into those cerulean pools
Sighing a sympathetic offering of stealth
I saw the look in his eyes and there looking back was myself.

Mind Part 2

Sat upright in a bed that's not your own, you syphon through packets of medication. You study each pill, piercing the foil carefully, listening to each pop, placing them delicately in your palm. They build and build until you cannot hold any more without them slipping from between your fingers and so you start to put them in your mouth. Powdery and metallic in taste, you let them fur on your tongue. You clench down your teeth.

Swallow.

There is no method here, no meditation, no ideal or thought-out end. You just do. You swallow and swallow and swallow until you feel your eyes pulse distorted black shapes onto the wall in front of you. What are you doing? You're not sure. In its greatest irony this is the closest to alive you've felt in months. The power. The power that you'd thought these very things had taken from you now reclaimed in a moment of adrenaline-filled weakness. Your fingers and toes shake furiously, your heartbeat in your ears, your stomach dropping from higher storeys with each breath. You try so desperately to close your eyes, pushing your back slowly down the middle of the bed but they're forced open. Stapled. Prized and widening with fear. What have you done? How did you get here? Why?
No answer sizzles to the surface, just aggressive acid reflux. Vomit. Most of it down your top and stuck in your hair. Nonplussed you are still here. Then, tears. Duvet-gagged screams. Anxious pleading text messages to recipients of such absurdity as you've forgotten who you have. If anyone might care. You stay awake for days. Leaving early in the morning you close the front door halfway as to not wake anyone and you slip off to a shopping centre. Zombie-like fingering through clothes that just hours ago you tempted to never wear again, you buy

them all. Dresses, make-up, books. Laden with distraction. Eyes still pulsing. Body tested to its final limits. Still working. Still pushing. Still alive. You arrive home silent. Curtains drawn, own bed. Two slices of dry toast. Vomit, again. You wriggle down and shut your eyes. Inner monologue shouting verses of your stupidity, angry and abusive phrases others have given you stuck to your mind's tongue, spitting it back as though it's language you have bred. It's not. Your phone vibrates. Anxiety. You haven't dared to read the things that you had sent. The panic of others' worry. The fear of who you may have hurt in hurting yourself. The gross indulgence of asking for help from someone so removed. Expecting someone to care. Your body writhes around in filth and shame. It is not until now that you realise what you've done. The weight of it all. The seriousness. This act of punishment administered so nonchalantly that it evokes terror each time you remember it. Why did it feel so innate? Why was it so easy? If no obvious trigger, who's to say the same again is not a sleepwalk away.

You open the message, it reads:

The reality you experience in your head is secondary and biased. You are a beautiful and awakened young woman, you are valuable and bright.

Hope. Heart-banging hope. Help. Hell driven to it.
Weightless and alive again, if only for a moment.
Days that follow are shamed and long, you take up running to exhaust you.
More messages, same sender. Loud and authoritative, tender and persistent.
Nobody else knows where your brain has taken you but them. But you are here now, unmasked, accounted for, being pulled forward by a rope of desperate late night slobbering calls that

without, you would have autopilot-slumped on the cold porcelain of a public bathroom.

There is not a night that passes where the words exchanged don't help you. Ease you. Humanise you. They cradle your battered brain to vow you will do the same for someone else at any cost. In your greatest weakness, they battled for your strength. You are here now, unmasked, accounted for, alive.

Inner Gold

Soften the shards
That broke you clean
Fresh and angry
As though they seem
Can be rounded as gems
Handed as souvenirs
To those who are yet to find light
In your old rotten fears.

Resilience

Novelty is such the mind's addiction
Cravings for comfort
In things that breed emptiness
Feasting on feelings with the unfriendliest
faces
But what if we traded to take from different places?
If we nourished our souls in ways we deserved
And picked softer tools to tickle our nerves
Cradled our minds in a sip of a sauce of its own brilliance
And found novelty in our mind's own source of resilience.

Dysthymia

It is uncomfortable blunt language
No apology screens sincere enough
For the screams and swearing
Of what it's made me do
It circles on my tongue
Bitter furs and tangs of acid
As I repent on how this thing
That I lost the remote for
Could ever make you feel
I didn't love you
In the deepest way I could.

Wrong Spaces

Why does the guilt
Always hit so late?
Twist and rip
It breaks me in two
Still not half enough
Still too whole
To dive back into
Dizzying nausea
Fills me up more and
More
Spurting, bursting
All encompassed hurting
Still not half enough
Still too whole.

Kindness

All that matters is kindness
I know it sounds obvious
But it's true
Think of all the bad things in the world
And then think of you
Think about all of the troubles you've faced
And then think of all the kind faces
That pulled you through
It's them that reminded you of your power
And on the days you feel you've got little purpose
Remember as humans it's as basic as showering
Others with kindness
Compassion
Lashings
Of love
Regardless of race, sex, location, and material stuff
It's kindness in its simplest sense
That will take us from this dark present
Into a more hopeful, prospecting tense.

Your Mind Is Biased

Your mind is biased
And your brain is blind
There's still a store of

                        strength

Left in you to find.

Worth

(written age 15)

Maybe we could've been friends
And I rushed us being lovers
Or I just knew deep down
That I was worth more than you having others.

Timestop / Heartstop / Fullstop

(written age 16)

You stepped in on your own fate
Having made me wait
You could've just let it be
But instead you made me late
For my own.

She Must

Be F̶at

dealing with
disordered eating,
body dysmorphia and
being born in the 90's

Body Part 1

It's April in London and you're smiling at your feet. Toes jumping up and down gently, padding against the leather sole of wicker wedges. It's your first day of your first job and the first time you've ever ordered a coffee. 'Two skinny chai lattes please.' A blonde woman, far too pretty to be fair, swings on her heels and reaches for a wooden swizzling stick. She looks like she's got her shit together, she's thin and tall and blonde and beautiful
and thin
and thin
and thin.

She's so thin.

You wish you could stand in that frame, all collarbones and angled elbows, but you're on the wrong side of 5'9" with rounded thighs and a well-cushioned overhang of tummy pressing out from your jeans. You squish it back in, smooth out your ponytail and walk half a block to work.

Everything is a clinical white, the walls, the backdrops, the shiny Apple Mac mouses, the lights, everything down to the people and their skin and the cyclical noise of clacking shoes. You pick up the arm of a steamer and rush it over a crimson satin dress, tickling the long sleeves down its seams and knock on the dressing room door. Nervous. 'Yah, I'm ready.'
It's her and it's you, her and her long-limbed body – naked from the waist up, tiny pert boobs meeting your eyes like pins pricking balloons. She places her left hand on your forearm to balance, steps into the dress, and waits for you to zip it at the back.

When you get home you unzip yourself.

Knickers snake the legs of jeans that lay atop a faded Marks & Spencer's bra, the underwire poking to catch the cuffs of your old favourite jumper. You drop your jewellery – weightless coppered rings that have left green replacements, thin golden chains, a hair clip pushing back your sweaty fringe. Off. Just in case. Deep sigh, deeper breath out. You arch your back forwards, you've forgotten your socks. Ankles embrace and tango to fling them off in a finale. Hopeful. Palms, cradling your stomach, there is more to give. 'Have a quick wee.' Just in case, deep sigh, deeper breath out, hopeful. Standing as a body, rosacea and bruises that paint Rorschach marks across the backs of your goose-pimpled thighs, just pure, finite flesh, your toes lift and tip with trepidation from bathroom tile to the familiar cold white skin of the scales. A number flashes and flits, undecided, jumping between aggressive differences, innocent to the wait of the worth and the worth of the weight. Static digits. Staring. There is more to give. There is more to understand. There is more to remembering the woman with the coffees and the girl and her naked body, there is more to you than what you think there should be less of. But still, as weeks turn over months and these moments feel like impressing years, you forget again in these alone minutes and all you know of yourself is a number.

Stuff

I think the thing that really gets me
The thing that turns me green
      The thing that makes me really want to scream
Is if I took away the inches
The measurements, the weight
The half-cut-up potatoes
Left to grow cold on my plate
The thing that makes me angry
Makes me want to cry
Is I've always been much smaller
Than the way I've understood size

I've made up sticks of butter
That I've told myself I'm made of
And I've sold myself as bigger
Arched my arms wider than needed to cradle
This magnificent piece of magic
That keeps me all together
This stuff that I have pulled at
This stuff that I should've treasured
This stuff that in all these years
I've told myself is huge
Has simply been the shape
Of the holiest refuge
With every time I look back
Sometimes only just a year
I wonder why I waddled with
This disgusting faulting fear
There was not that much of me
There was just enough
There was cellulite and thighs
But there was also just this stuff

This stuff that wasn't ugly
This stuff that wasn't big
This stuff that was simply just me
Stretching to a woman from a kid
This stuff that I don't remember
Ever wishing there wasn't less of
But as I'm getting older
I can't stand it being the death of
My sense of reality
I only hope
I only pray
I'll start to see
If I look properly
There'll never be too much of me.

Shoreditch House

She took one look at me and decided not to change her dress
Decided that even in her work clothes
They'd still serve further to impress
Him
The depression has started to kick in
I slipped in
To this
I slip into this
I slip in every time
She'll kiss him
Without changing her dress
And I'll kid her I'm still fine.

Kale

Oh Kale leaves
How you depress me
I only eat you
So boys want to
Undress me.

Kale Reprised

(two years later)

I've been eating a lot of chips
To fill out the dips in my hips
That your fingers used to press
Nothing but a starving urge
To spill out of the silhouette
You'd once undress.

Wrigley's Extra

The comparison's a killer
So much so it's gum for dinner
Why didn't god birth me thin

The god I love lives in this house
She's beautiful
But the god I hate force fed my mouth
With words about my figure
That's why tonight it's gum for dinner

I say god
But the voice isn't holy
It's the voices of memories
Of boys who shuddered to hold me
Strange men in the street who scolded me
Inner thoughts who offered me
Biscuits when I was sad not hungry
That's why tonight it's gum for dinner

Perhaps I've got the wrong idea
Praying to someone who isn't here
For more lithe limbs and straighter hair
Bowing solemnly to such unfair words
Because if he was real, he'd be a sinner
He couldn't last on gum for dinner

He'd have no power in his bones
His voice would shout in shadowed tones
And pass out before he could complain
The confliction of this strength for weakness
Has always driven me insane.

Trump

This was written pre his presidency and the naivety that hoped his voice wasn't one that ~~caused~~ resonated is still painful

Tell me, sir
Explain it loud and clear
Shout your most direct
Explicit fears
Scream them until
The decibels reach parallel
To the clang and clatter in my heart
Until you can rage each syllable
So pointedly you can throw your voice like a sharpened dart
And throw it for me
Speak for me
Times those fears by ten
Then times them by one hundred
And one thousand and again
Keep multiplying what shakes you
Until it becomes so monstrous
So tangible and noxious
That it no longer feels like fear
It just feels constant
Familiar
Monotonous
Like you've spent your life rehearsing
For a nightmare
As the understudy
Never quite enough for the part
Because you don't qualify as somebody
Like you've learnt every line
As though what you feel is fiction
And you'll never get the lead as someone
Whose script is written with conviction

Tell me, sir
Explain it loud and clear

Explain it so loudly my unborn daughter can hear
Project your voice into the future
If you can impregnate me with these lost morals
You're free to rape me just as quick
And then what happens if you conceive more than fear?
What happens if I don't want that kid?
Your future is bubble-wrapped
And I'm held punishable for it.
Try and tell me that you're scared
As you bang my head on the glass ceiling
And drag me by my hair
Through statements like
SHE ASKED FOR IT
I'm pretty sure I didn't ...
Pretty sure I'm pretty more
Than a pretty face to be ignored

Tell me, sir
Explain it loud and clear
Because I'm lost
Wandered down too many paths
With no roads for me safe enough to cross
Without carrying my keys like a weapon
Been employed in too many places
Where I'm a disposable body on a ladder to step on
Tell me, sir
Mr, why are your Mrs'
Missing out?
Why do you consider us so little?
Who was the man that taught you
To grow into this man so bitter
Dishing out
What I can and cannot be?
Who was the man that showed you a lesser being
And why was that lesser being me?

Filters

My eyes a little brighter
My teeth a little whiter
My skin a little clearer
And my hair
...accidentally a little greener
The contrast of the exposure
Is not one that's clearer
The definition of the portrait
Is one of a heavyweight
Photoshopper
VSCO-er
I feel pretty when I'm told I am
I feel petty when it's as cold as
I'm a barefaced liar
#NoFilter filter
A scared-faced beauty in disguise
A normal looking human being
But my profile picture has you surprised
As though it's an image I'd been dreaming
The resemblance is close
My jawline is still mine
And my nose is still my nose
But would I still be of anyone's desire
If I wasn't hidden behind Instagram's required
Mask?
The mask of a fool
The mask of the twenty-first-century cruel world
Or the mask of a self-conscious tryna be cool girl
Does it matter?
I still sit and pixelate
Digitally deliberate, curl into an aesthetic looking ball
Until my anxiety is a candidate for Britain's Next Top face of
     the intimidated

My idea of beauty was once so different
So why have I confined that wonder
Into an ugly 4x4 square of imprisonment?
That has parameters smaller than the size of my thighs and is
    duller than the natural gradient of my eyes
I sit back so often with a chest thudding sigh
Scrolling
Refreshing
Relentless tapping
All down to an art
And think
Since when did I ignore my own heart to hack at my own life?
And since when did I become an image to sell of a millennial
    with scraps of sanity as its price?

London Pervs

I swear to god
I'll swear louder than the tops
Of my stretched swollen lungs
I'll scream 'til I'm blue
And tie knots in your slimy shallow tongues
I swear to god
It's quite a simple thing to grasp
That if you shout at me in the street
Or brush your hand against my arse
If you simmer me down to a piece of meat
I won't be the one falling to their knees
Put your whistles in your pockets
Force your eyes back in their sockets
Spin your heels and curve your tongues into a curl
I will only say this once so listen up:
You've *picked* the wrong girl.

Women's Tea

I went into a health food store
To buy some spring roll skins
And found myself instead
In an aisle of loose leaf tea tins

Digestion, anxiety, whatever your ailment
They were stacked in dozens of varieties
And foreign flagrant flavours

This one box caught my *eye*
Barbie brash bold pink
It read 'Women's Tea'
And I was lost on what to think
Stuff the patriarchy!
Stuff your colour-denoted sexes!
When were leaves vulnerable to this malarkey!
I bet it's even more expensive

So I marched with echoed stomps
And slammed it on the desk
Turns out some herbs are good for cramps
And some are good for men

So I pocketed my placards
And zipped my coat over my Pankhurst shirt
And thought before I spluttered statistics
I should have a cuppa first.

Imposter

I have always thought
That people have commented on
My beauty
Because of my female appearance
As though my gender was a given
For physical applause
But never did I realise
That it could be because they found me beautiful
And yet when it's been suggested
That I'm not in proportion
I have felt unworthy
Of this gender at all
And panic unsure
In a male gaze
That tips me on a scale
Of which I always weigh too heavy
To know what's true.

Hunger

Weighted by the weight of me
Weightless when I quickly eat
Forgetting all the bits I see
In the bathroom, only me
At the table I transport
To somewhere that I can't be caught
Ham-fisted with empty calories

Picking plates, pushed pieces
Straightened back, stretched out creases
Knife and fork, balanced crossed
Brain salivating into figures lost
What deliciousness it forces, fake
As the satiation is a masked empty
That is only weighted by the weight of me.

Gift For A Man

I'm scared that if things don't change
If I don't shout louder
I'll be met with a future daughter
Who will feel a pressure on her worth to shrink shorter
And I'll be responsible if I have to hear her say:

'How can I be so foolish
to sit with marble ham thighs
A masculine tone
Dilated pupils and tar-stained bone
And think someone might wish
Upon each passionate gesture I make
I might be his to kiss?'

Fingers that bend all but the middle
Dirtied language and eyes of white
Stand to a halt as each stranger approaches her at night
And as she struggles to find the compliment
It's their lurid advances that give her a twisted confidence

That no matter how tall she stands
She'll only be worthy of love
If she kneels, plain and thin
As a gift for a man.

How will I make her feel something new
When I've spent so much time feeling that that might be true?

Sobriety

This present day
Has no tonic to dilute it
Uncarbonated calm
Eyes wide awake
That stare down old habits
Searching out new ones
Somewhat disappointed
To find present day.

Cellulite (Sells You Heavy)

There is a fold beneath the crease
That haunts me with trepidation
And despite what preparation
Goes into each breakfast
It seems there is an infiltration
This breeding nation
Of fat
That crawls and creeps between my legs
Regardless of what weight I shed
The bicycle motions I do in bed
Are relentless
Where is the redemption
For those who exercise?
My thighs
Jesus Christ the size
It should not be fair
Cellulite, sells you heavy
Cells from genes I was not ready to grow
Jeans that are unable to grow with me
They exhaust me from the source of me
They heckle me from each freckle on me
And if I could take a biological eraser
Remove these frustrating chubby placers
I thought I would
I tried to tell myself each dimple is a smile along my skin
A lightning bolt breaking from within
The happiness of a chicken nugget
Is a small white rocket
That bends to be a part of me
Pretends to be a piece of me
But nothing that small can be the defeat of me
And that's why I stopped wishing them away

I can't tell you how free it feels to prod them
And be okay
To look at them and be fine
To open up and say
My body stretched to make this space
And these tiny imperfections are mine.

This is the first poem
I posted on facebook.
People loved it.
I hate still how I
lied. I'd not yet found
peace - I just didn't know
how to share something
so painful,
without the fear of being
shamed.

Fat

Please
I beg you
Don't touch that
That handle that you want to grab
That protruding piece of mass
Please don't touch that
Don't remind me of my dinner
Then absolve your arms as though I am thinner
Please don't touch that

Please don't touch that and then pretend it isn't there
Yet still give me an unapproving stare
When I reach for seconds
Please, I'm asking nicely
Don't touch that even politely
Don't laugh at all my icons
And say I could be her if my thighs were gone
If my legs were tight and long
Please don't touch that

Don't command my skin like you are proud
When publically you are loud
About how there's too much
But somehow in bedroom whispers
Your language dissolves straight into touch
Please don't touch that
If you can't see it's me
I have spent too many years
Stroking my own thigh to knee
To know what's there
And if for a sober second
Deep within your heart's compassion

You think you might have capacity
To hesitate my weight and then scream sexual passion

Please for the love of god don't touch that

Don't touch me at all

Because I spend too much time weighing myself

To wait to see that you're such a fool

To touch me

And not see the pain that's looking back

Don't touch me when you know how I feel and you call that
feeling fat

Please don't touch that.

Body

He touches you. *He* is no one in particular in your recollection, he has become many faces. Faces that interchange within your memory upon recalling any which one of these stories you begin to tell your friends and then retreat. You say nothing. Your face grows depressed at the concept and with your same face you feel disgusting. As hands paw along your flesh you are so aware of all that you are. How that might be unattractive. How if it feels uncomfortable to you, how grotesque it must feel from the palms of another. Past experience has told you this anxiety is worthy. Past faces have furrowed eyebrows and then widened and pursed lips to disgruntle at the space within which you take up. You push it from your brain. Relax. Remember to relax. Remember that the reason why you have a disjointed relationship with your body is because you can't relax. But you can't. Popping candy synapses wet between your ears and fire off all manner of heart spasms and unease and short breaths and weighted defeat.

He asks you to say things, to do things.
You say them, you do them.

In the same instance that you choose not to remember his name, because he has had so many, you choose not to remember the list of bursting speech bubbles that blew from between your lips with syruped saliva, and even though they are old, they sound new, and even in your memory, you say them again.

Dutifully.

This, surely, is how you relax.

Listening, observing, serving. Taking action and control from someone more confident, more experienced. You let him touch you, your body shivers with an immoderate buzz of panic that he confuses for excitement, quietly disguising against your own will, relearning your own body. These are not mixed messages, this is the only language that you know. Quietly in inner turmoil. Nothing here is obvious or certain. It's just uncomfortable. But that's how it always is and how it's always been and you are sure will always be and the reason why you feel so disconnected and afraid and ashamed of this experience is because all that he's touching, all that he's grabbing already distastefully is

Fat.

You feel every inch of yourself squirm. Suddenly everything is obvious and everything is certain.

Everything is wrong.

You are stuck in the flash of your own realisation, hands reaching for duvet, fingers being bent back upon themselves with his.

His pace quickens and you assume a noise to the action, you heard it once in a film your friend's older brother showed you, a stale but stuck reference point, so you echo it. Echo, echo, echo. You find yourself here time and time again, telling yourself that you're putting yourself through exposure therapy, telling yourself you deserve it, telling yourself this is good, telling yourself *this is normal*, this is normal, you have put yourself here, you have been complicit this far, ignore why, ignore your discomfort, ignore the fact you realised this on the journey here and you've since tried to leave and you've asked to leave, you've asked politely and then you've said bluntly and then you've booked a cab and then it's been cancelled, but your brain is so heavy with hate and self-doubt and confusion that you've forgotten you've said those things. You've forgotten he's noticed, you've forgotten he's said no to your no, you've forgotten he's played into your weakness. You've forgotten who you are. So you listen to his rhetoric and tell yourself that your body will be yours to own once someone has put a price on it that you're willing to buy it back for. But you never seem to. You never want to buy it back because it is offered in such unrecognisable packaging, that you hope the last transaction means it's yours no longer.

'Please, please, just take me. Take it all from me and let me no longer be responsible.'

Your responsibility feels excruciating and complicated and exhausted. You had tried so many times to free your body but now it's all so enmeshed you're lost for how.

You're lost. You're tired. You're vulnerable. Unknowingly, because of those things, your brain is whimpering on behalf of your body:

'Please, please, just take me. Take it all from me and let me no longer be responsible.'

Until one day a man does, in a way that you feel is absolute, that feels so concrete, he takes it in such a way that it is no longer yours to bargain with. He stamps on it. You have been here before but until this moment you don't realise the danger. He touches your fat body and tells you what it is, he drags it, tells you he's caressing, and no matter how many times you question it in your head, question it aloud, say you are tired, say you are asleep, actually fall asleep, dream vivid nightmares prematurely, wake up and feel his breath inhale your protests, he hands back half the worth that's half the worth of what you were afraid of that you owned. Nobody knows, you never mention it. Just him. Just you. In retrospect, just all of you. Just a night where you entered a room feeling fat and left feeling much heavier. You wonder for months, 'Would this have happened if I was skinny and confident and could just say no?' And one day you hope, it's still not yet, you can turn around and see that you'd always said no, and one day you'll see that no rolls or cellulite can count as witnesses, not because it wasn't true, but because they weren't there.

Bodies

You can turn them off and on
You can make them fat then thin
You could do a lot of courageous stuff
If we gave them enough space to breathe in
The prodding is an obvious hurdle
And the feeling your stomach feels
When it's near ready for its contents to curdle
The thighs leaning back
Trying to impression a gap
Waiting for a waistline
To waste away
It's all a trap
Squeezing anxiously at your face
And your nail beds being the last thing that you could taste
Wondering if down there is tight enough
Wondering if your jaw line is slight enough
Enough
These bodies that we've made
Are much stronger than we ever knew
Before we saw what we'd face
They're bigger than our thoughts
And sturdier than our psyche
It's a miracle that they can't speak
Because if they could they'd shout
WHY CAN'T YOU JUST LIKE ME
I'm doing so much stuff
That you don't ever see
I'm forcing organs and beating breaths
I'm keeping us alive, quietly
                    And all you do is complain
What's sad is it's fair and often contrite
We do all of this personal grieving

Even though we know that it's not right
But how we can we change our learnt perceptions
When the thoughts that we breed are invited to receptions
Daily
To listen to our own lack of worth
When our bodies are trailed through media's dirt
When school is not about grades but the length of your skirt
If I'm half a size smaller will I be liked first
I've only had liquids so how do I quantify thirst
When sex isn't about love but 'how much did it hurt?'
When do we remember our worth
It really is worth it
To think about how we're working
Not to fixate on the vanity parade
That we're constantly scrolling and old school surfing
This stuff we consume is so fleeting
When there's stuff that supports us a whole life time
That keeps us breathing
And we shun it
Tell us in a lottery of bodies
Everyone else has won it
But us
That's crazy
        Crazy that we fill ourselves with so little that we're hazy
We can't think properly
Because our diets are so light
That our concentration's sloppy
That our skin is so grim
Because we drink ourselves so wobbly
Our head bangs so bad that we can't help but think somberly
We're chain smoking at the sight of a sky
So you can just pause for a moment
And on your own sigh 'what's wrong with me?'
That is not a good use of a body

It should be angry and charging
Not knackered and starving
It has so much power to be starting
Anything we drive it towards
Past a distraction of how we treated it before
Past us ignoring its own personal encore
To be reignited
For the love of whatever is good
What the hell are we fighting?
When the skin we're in
Holds us closer than our next of kin
Ever could
Why are we fighting against something
That gods never would?
Why are we bowing to a new fate
That our muchness is weighed up to
To the weight that we weigh
That our sumptuous ethereal smart humanness means
We'll always think we are paupers
But have the same bodies as queens

I Am Not Yours To Be Beautiful

I am not yours
To be beautiful for
I do not clothe myself
To be adored
The most finite of Knowledge
That I can keep steady
Is that I am mine
To feel sexy.

She Must

~~Be an Adult~~

Twenty two —
dealing with too
          much —
about to deal with
<u>MVCH</u> worse.

Age

You are eight years old, tiny toes and fingers have clambered up onto the sofa and sprawled, soft head first, onto the lap of your grandfather. You unpick a packet of Chewits cautiously, popping a pink one in your mouth and clammy handedly produce a yellow one for him. In between each chomp he smiles

> 'One day you'll be as old as me,
> I never knew I'd be as old as me.'

It frightens you. Your eyes close and you sigh. He pauses, rushes his hands through your hair and grins

> 'Think of all the adventures you're going to have. I wonder who you'll marry? I wonder if that man has been born yet, where is he in the world? I wonder who you'll decide to be. Isn't that exciting! You just don't know yet but I know it's all going to be brilliant.'

It sticks with you much longer than he ever let it be a thought. It sticks with you until those questions grow around your ribs and seep into your lungs, you push them out past sighs and lengthen them to breaths. You let them grow to become place holders for answers.

Your mother and your grandmother sit across from you on that same sofa, you are now fourteen. The dips and peaks of their profiles are identical to yours, their fidgets mirror, their breaths beat similar. You think of all the adventures they've had, the mistakes they've made and the promises they've kept. The women they've become. The powerhouses and strong-willed statues, the no-nonsense and all loving, the triers and succeeders, the women.

You open up the place holders your grandfather first created and stamp them there as quotation marks, these are the women you too will become. Growing up, in that pause, is suddenly less daunting.

But before you know it it's 3 a.m. on a Monday and you're typing cover letters with one hand and spoon feeding yourself baked beans on penne pasta from your bed, there is an old soup stain on your top making friends with a much older red wine stain, there is chipped nail varnish on your veneers from gnashing, forty-three unread text messages, fifteen new Tinder matches and one series of Master of None replaying over and over on an infinite loop in the background. The room smells tired. You fall asleep, everything left in its place.

Four hours later, in your mother's blazer and your grandmother's dress, shoes that your father once bought you and a necklace you 'borrowed' from somebody else's jewellery box, a little girl looks up at you with her pearl drop eyes of hope and wonder, unstuck momentarily from the moving landscape out the commuter train window and she surveys you. You smile at her as your ovaries trick you with a pang. She nestles her face behind her hands and takes another peek through her digits. She is wary. She looks at you, really looks, gaze fixated, and sees you, wholesomely, as an adult. When did this happen? It all happened so fast. And did it really happen at all? You want to shake her, lift off your blazer and show her your pyjama top still worn underneath, pull out the small bunny rabbit toy that you hide in your handbag for comfort, read her the panicked text messages to your mother that scream

I don't know how to be an adult.

Scroll through countless photos of you in Ladbroke Grove just last week with red eyes and greasy hair, ham-fisted with receipts from a drunken hotel night stay, empty packets of cigarettes splayed across the table, searching for loose change to get the train to work, to get this train to work. 'Shit, I'm going to work.'

Shit, I'm an adult and nobody told me.

Goldman
Sachs

Sometimes it doesn't go right
The wayward nights
You imagined
The taxi trips with strangers
Paying bar bills with party favours
Sometimes it isn't a film
No vignette close enough
To cradle you within
Its dark expanse and tell you that
Not all of these men want adventure
Not all of them are character studies
Not all of them think you're funny and smart
Not all of them want to hear about your father
Not all of them want to be a consensual partner
Sometimes it doesn't go right
And sometimes it's best
To go home and straight to bed
Instead of exploring the night.

I'll Be Home In The Morning

This is a mistake
But something in my loins says yes
Something allows him to undress
Something takes me straight to bed
And that something doesn't live in my head
It sits a pain within my chest
Beyond a place where secrets rest
It's dark and I don't like it there
It's packed with secrets and overstuffed
Yet what it screams that mutes me deaf
The most blatant entry I misread
Says simply:

Don't do this
When all you want to be is loved.

Too Young

It drizzled down
Precious and thin
Weaving matted through my hair
My neck crooked over the side of the bath
And your shoes gone from the bottom of the stairs.
I must've been
Only fifteen
But that nausea was centuries old
My nose plugged with the scent of your cheap aftershave
And the shower head spitting out cold
You said I no longer tasted much like love
And my hips were the wrong side of wide
I tried to wash you like dirt from off my red mottled skin
And let you sink with the suds down the pipes
But you left a scum that stuck to the sides.

Say You're Sorry

She was nearly my age
When she first heard your name
It will take until her age
For me to walk away
And now at your age
Everything's too late.

They Came Out And I Stayed In

All my friends are gay
And I wouldn't have it any other way
Except on Friday nights
When I've got no one to get off with.

E1W 3SS/Billy

Come up
And come down with me
Taste your figures
On the furs of your teeth
Youth might be wasted on the young
But slip into this neon vulnerability
And we'll be wiser when the morning comes
That ravages on our undressed mess
But sip on the warm-ending edges of the sleepless sun
And we'll be wiser before we're wasted again
On all the thoughts we slurred and acted on
Come up
And come down with me

We can't do this when we're thirty.

Pint-Sized

I've got this thing with kids on trains
I sit there mesmerised
Watching the silhouettes of flashing landscapes
Reflect like magic in their eyes
Watching their tiny bodies perform
Pint-sized
Attempts at behaving
Swaying
With each stop

I'd quite like to swap

Because I can't remember anymore
Of how it felt to take up such little space
And for that to be a good thing
For my learning and naivety
Grabbing hands and misused words
To be a sweet thing
How it felt to be a glaring honest thing
I wish back then I would have taken note

Could've scraped together all the statements I didn't know to
        sugar coat
And kept them in my armour
Kept their tangy sour taste and smile at them with the
        same charm
A new little girl now has
With my old grabbing hands
I want to shake her to realize
That her mischief is perfect
And that growing up is a downsize
Just stay put,
And only move as the train moves.

WhatsApp

In these times
Of double ticks
Last seen minutes
And ghosting pricks
Just text your girls
And save your breath.

Roots Of Them/Sorry, Jacob

They're so beautiful
And even when I feel not so
They still remain
And there's a beauty in knowing
That when it can't be self-proclaimed
It can still be breathed in, seen and attained
That those around you's beauty always escapes your change
Well sort of, same same
But different
You see it as a caged reminder of wrongdoings
An unmeasurable imprisonment
It thrashes a hotter whip
Lashes of a slobbering trip
As you lick your lips
And taste the saltiness of their beauty
Instead of smelling it as sweet
Sometimes the feelings we mistake
As a clarity on others darkness
Screaming solemn swears that
The harmless are heartless
Is us projecting our fear of losing beauty
Of power, of wonderment, of worth
But for what it's worth
What I've learnt
Is to swallow it down and accept it

Pick up a tougher smile as you exit
Pick up what you admire and inspect it
Until you understand why you respect it
Take time to realise the roots of them are the roots of you
And you'll think yourself beautiful too.

Kids

Our bones stuck like honey
Silken gestures grazing ground
As we flew over handlebars
And relished in dotting our bloodied scars with the same tiny
    digits that made shapes with carbon-backed stars.
The nonsense made sense in its cherry-rich taste of speaking a
    language of pulling funny faces.
The fear of inferior was nothing but a shifting canvas that smelt
    like summer
Shedding our winter skin to become a
Firecracker of innocence
An uncorrupted, feverishly disruptive
Blazing ball of wonder
And when we expanded from its amber shell
Spitting sparks as we embraced the swell
Each filament of learning spun a grand farewell
And spoke a greeting to the less bright
Other side of where those taller weren't glowing
I'm sure we'd never have grown up if
We'd been told where we were going.

Forever

Can you be related to a soulmate?
Can you be born into fate?
Can two nodding identical profiles
Bear such growing worldly weight?
I sympathise my all
With those who need to find the one
When all of my searching
Stopped when I begun
Because the child in me has always known
The only one I need
Will always be my mum.

Baby Ella

Fingernails flat like scraps of seashells
Pull and paw at a tide of softness
Scratching out unthought feelings
Human hieroglyphics
Of maternity
As these tiny digits cling to me
Until I breathe out a shape of my heart
And imagine it as your own
No longer frightened
Knowing that all that's within me
Hands like yours one day
Will hold and call home.

Adult

You are shoulder to someone's waist in rows of black. A ceiling above you fifteen times as many feet as you stand and as ornate and detailed as the Skechers trainers you'd begged to wear today but had been denied. Mum said they were inappropriate. You didn't know what that meant. They were black and silver, just the same in your mind's eye as every outfit you'd ever seen in Disney shows that were worn to funerals. You take a pew, bashfully battle your lungs for song and try to ignore the sobs. Grief is an unexplored, unexplained alien that greets you at a coffin, offers out its hand in introduction and pulls away quick enough for you to remain unacquainted properly. You go to offer it small talk but it is already someone else's turn. You sit at a wake and watch people get drunk, laugh and tell stories, cry quietly safe in the knowledge that you, a small child who knows nothing, is only watching. There is something inside of you that begs to feel sad, to understand. You pull and push for tears, fists banging against your eyes to see stars, wishing for water but nothing comes. You feel your age for the very first time in a way that you'll always remember. You are eight. You feel young. You feel untainted. You feel like today is a controlled blip in the universe being driven by a car that will keep on going to a place where you'll never have to return. You only need to stand at this place once. You tell yourself, despite your known and sure naivety, with such total confidence that today is not normal and will not ever have to happen again. The world that you know is not made to allow for such capacity for sadness. The world that you know is so new it cannot end.

Ten years later, then eleven and twelve, you put on a dress that is black and a necklace that is silver, you have tried on eight different things still not knowing what is appropriate. You always end up in the same dress. You settle, smooth it down, you cry. You have been to many of these now, you even know the words to hymns you proudly once shrugged off. Everything hurts and yet everything is weightless.

Almost too close to feeling the blood run and rush away from your body, almost lifeless, but flowing into a room that is pulsing and cursing that it's still alive and desperately attempting to meditate around the idea that being here, portrait not horizontal, is a lucky thing. None of you feel lucky. All of you wish just for a moment you were horizontal. You feel grief.

It smacks you soberly until you reach for a glass and engage in a chat that brings you to reminiscing. Only recounting the good things. Feeling your soul filled with countless anecdotes about a person you wished you had called and retold with them but now you can't. Everyone pretends that what others share is special but only what they share is special to them because they can't share it with the only person that would laugh loudest, who knows every face in the room, because they aren't also holding a glass. They're not pressed up on the bar side, or holding your hand after school, or silently judging your hangover. They're gone, replaced with a silhouette of grief.

Days after, every time, you feel much older. Much wiser. So much taller than the child that once only wished for sparkly trainers and a car that kept on revving. You feel, for the first time, again and again, like an adult. Growing up becomes not of broken romances, not of grades, not of jobs, not of pounds of flesh or those in the bank and not of expectations. It even, for a moment, that flits subconsciously, is not of trying to stay alive, not of thinking back on all the times you had pondered or tried to not be. It's of being purposeful. Of making so goddamn sure that when your time comes there are stories and laughter, that there are people who know they were loved, that there were successes to recount, that there was advice that was shared, that there were parties and chats and changes. That whatever room at whatever time you leave deaf, you are certain that you know if you could hear anything at all, that what is walked out beside you and what is spluttered and sobbed and sung generously, is that you had love and that you had purpose.

Months after, those sentiments seem trivial again, almost forgotten in the ether of everyday life, of recovery and acceptance. It's your birthday. You are standing on a chair, holding the hems of a dress your younger self would have dreamt of and you say, simply and so drunkenly it's almost incoherent, 'Thank you all for being here, thank you for giving me the life I have, I love you.' You step down to walk away as people whoop and cheer and laugh and grin and chink their glasses until you can float to the back of the bar and cry.

The funny thing in all of this, the thing so funny it's often quite difficult to find laughable, is the banality of everything you feel in what initially comes at you with such a distinguished pang as though it'll never come again, but it does. It does and it does and it does. It keeps on smacking your brain with a heavy punch that suggests you weren't expecting it until you start to study it. Until there it is again, that feeling, that anxiety, that kiss, that argument, and so you involuntarily laugh once your head bruise has simmered down to nearly skin colour and you roll your eyes and let out this lip shaking smile of a giggle that's really a sigh. That moment of realisation, suddenly in your twenties, that the last ten years have been on a cyclical calendar of emotion. Heartbreak, terror, grief, unworthiness, fatness, stupidity, relief, euphoria. You still have absolutely no idea what to do with them, what accent they speak with until you've heard them again, what weight they hold until they're thrust upon you, what bellowing bone-cringing laugh of a noise that will seep from within the depths of your lungs once the end of the loop comes round again and you realise.

You realise the most marvellous thing, the most life-affirming, presence- keeping bit of it all, is you're absolutely definitely without a doubt not supposed to know how to feel or how to think upon those feelings, nobody else does around you either. Not even those who suggest they do and not even you on a Tuesday night with a glass of wine feeling philosophical and wise do. You're in this circuit now and the best you can do is give it a nod every time you re-recognise an old thought introducing itself as unstale. You've done it, really. The foundations are built. Now all that is left is to choose how you respond knowing how things turned out the last time you didn't know you had choice.

Seaweed – For Grandad

Before it was the future
Before it was my brain
Before it was gun reforms
Before it was climate change
Before it was heartbreak
Before it was potential
Before it was plastics in the sea
Before it was existential
Before it was family illness
Before it was personal tax
Before it was the price of houses
Before it was the price of a wax
Before I knew what really worried me

It was seaweed

Long gangly tendrils of green
Wefts of Medusa's very own wig, had you asked me
Evil slithery things
That clasped around my ankle
Left in the water by one of Poseidon's own vandals
My two innocent limbs braving a leisurely dangle
Until I decided the holiday was cut short
Because I was convinced I was up next to be strangled

Before it was my weight
Before it was purpose
Before it was societal standards
Before it was junior nurses
Before it was Donald Trump
Before it was dairy alternatives
Before it was the state of my skin

Before it was what state we're in with the Conservatives
Before it was 'What do you mean no WIFI?'
Before it was Twitter trolls
Before it was feeling like a fraud
Before it was over-ambitious goals

It was seaweed

Before it was the effects of contraception
Before it was terrorism
Before it was the end of Inception
Before it was faux feminism

It was seaweed
My first experience of the unknown
I ran sandy toed
Into the only arms I trusted
'Grandad!' I cried, flustered
'I can't go back in there!'
Frightened, I was pointing at the sea
Whilst he was laughing at me
Not in a way that I know now
No, he was giggling kindly
'Darling, it's just grass,
Come on, I'll show you.'
And he did that gorgeous thing
When as a kid adults pretend to throw you
And then catch you
And bring you back to their chest
And you sniff in a nuzzle
As they kiss your head

And everything melts away

All my worries were just bits of grass in the sea
All the hope that I needed was him smiling at me
All the knowledge I had
Had come from his brain
And despite all of my anxieties
That thought keeps me sane

Someone will always know more
Someone will always be grinning
Someone will always be willing
Someone will hold you
When it all seems too big
Someone will show you
The real size that it is
Yes, the world's scary
My god is it tough
But there will always be someone
Who loves you enough
To try and take it away
And that someone
Made you someone enough
To be your own someone
To make sure you're okay

Before it was seaweed
It was blissful and calm
But I'd cradle an ocean of watery weeds
To know that I'd always be safe in your arms.

Expectations

Am I soft enough
Am I tame enough for you?
Does my name taste sweet enough
Are my convictions lame enough for you?
Am I seen enough
And herded by you?
What is it to be a good woman
In a world of bitter truths?
Am I soft enough?
Am I half enough for you?

Yellow Cabs

I had always claimed
Regret could never know me
Regret could never drive me
I would not allow myself to wallow in his punishing fear

As I sit and count out my last quarters
He offers his hand to take them
Pocketing a shrapnel token
And taxis me to JFK.

Hospital Visits

No colour is quite its best self
Insipid yellows and half *greys*
Walls flake
With an old damp regret
Not yet brave enough to peel off entirely
The din of wheels and microwave meals
Clack and click unconfidently
And as your throat constricts
And you feel sick to your stomach
You can't help but wonder
If it's the grip of somebody else's death
Trying to talk to you.

You will choose to not give yourself the best chance. It will often not feel like a choice but an act of punishment. A self-declaration that you are not worthy of the good or the exciting, to feel proud or to feel smart or to feel good enough. You push away friendships that fulfil you and enter relationships that break you, you continue toxic cycles of bad habits and behave with such an aggressive recklessness that to those on the outside you seem a fool. A fool that doesn't care. But you do, you care so deeply that when you are full you feel you have no choice but to spit everything out. To excel in purging all that you are and all that you hate and all that you have and all that you love. It seems nonsensical in the brief and dark and tired moments of reflection. A reflection in which you cannot recognise the planes of your own face and the curves of your own mind.

In the end, it all boils down to these minutiae, these tiny fleeting moments, these vignettes. They all pass you by so quickly. Some of them feel as though they will, they feel as weightless as the seconds they are often administered in. But all considered and put together, these are what shape you. Pain you, excite you, almost break you. All just moments you thought could never be beaten in their insanity. Memories and makings of this jaggedy soul that may well be mad but is the greatest body of strength you'll ever know.

My rhetoric is changing
My need for love confused
I've lost my inner monologue
And sold it all for views.

Click To Accept The Terms and Conditions

Shout a little louder
Come a little closer
Let me lead you to the void
The blank expanse
Let yourself fly in a seat
That is pants
Boom across a room
That cares for you little
Wipe off a slick
Of your new hungry spittle
That we'll sell you as gold
Come grab a feel
Of a hand you can't hold
Come be a person
That you never knew
Feel grand and feel gorgeous
Then feel worthless and through
Take a trip down the tubes
Get settled in
Welcome, you've signed up
It's all about to begin.

Acknowledgements

Thank you to me for actually writing all of this even though most days have been cripplingly difficult and filled with self-doubt and, likely, laziness. Well done for getting your arse in gear, more of that please.

To Abigail Bergstrom, who courted me when I was a shy teenager who couldn't even look at her, to growing me into a woman who loves her career and loves telling people about it. I am forever indebted to you and all we've been through together.

To Lisa Milton at HQ, thank you for honouring me with the privilege of this journey from book to book, for championing women and fighting hard for our voices.

To Adrian, Ali, Steph, Katie, Laura, Richie, Lucy, Chris, Sean, Jackson, Jack and Finn – thank you for picking up the phone in the middle of the night, thank you for boozedays, thank you for holding me when I didn't know who 'me' was. Quite literally, ride or dies.

To Jon, I love you. I hope this is an accurate enough portrait of just how brilliant you are. I am so lucky to write about you and I will never take it for granted.

To Nigel and Angela, for welcoming me into your family so graciously, I love you.

To my darling Grandmother, for your strength and stay and a laugh that could get the world through anything.

To Mops, Pickles, Kermit, Stinky, Sloane and the goose. I couldn't do this without all of you.

And of course, to my Mum. Thank you for your unwavering support and love and understanding. You get the last word in everything I do. MORE.